Compassion for Animals as Christian Spirituality

EVERY CREATURE
a WORD *of* GOD

ANNIKA SPALDE
&
PELLE STRINDLUND

Vegetarian Advocates Press
Cleveland, Ohio

© 2008 Vegetarian Advocates Press
P.O. Box 201791
Cleveland, OH 44120

Vegetarian Advocates Press
Cleveland, Ohio

ISBN 978-0-9716676-3-1

Original Swedish publication: 2005
Swedish publisher: Arcus Förlag

Translated into English by: Joel Kilgour and Pelle Strindlund
Cover photo by: Hendrik Zeitler

— TABLE *of* CONTENTS —

THE SPIRITUAL JOURNEY

A POLICE CAR APPEARED in the oncoming lane. We held our breath. Had the alarm sounded? Were they looking for us? Should we each take a box and run into the woods?

It passed by our left. Maybe the officers saw our license plate. We checked the rearview mirror for the red glow of their brake lights – a sure sign that our mission would be over.

Did they brake? Not yet...

This is a book about being Christian in a world shared with other beings. We do not live here alone. We have brothers and sisters. "The animals," wrote the American monk Thomas Merton (1915–68), "are the children of God."[1] What does a spirituality that affirms God's love for all creatures look like? That is the central question of this book.

The animal rights movement is a recent development, but Christian concern for animals is not. We see it in the stories of medieval monks who helped hares and deer escape from hunters, and of desert hermits who offered water to thirsty donkeys.

In these pages you will discover the rich history of animal-friendly living and theology within the Christian tradition. Maybe you will be surprised by what some Bible passages have to say about human and animal relationships. We will offer you tools for reflection on how to follow Jesus today, at the beginning of the third millennium. This is also a book about the joy of living a value-driven life. We hope you will make the same discovery that we – and an increasing number of Christians around the world – have made: that God's mercy reaches beyond the borders of humanity.

After having spent a large part of our adult lives working with underprivileged people – from Asunción, Paraguay to Tyler, Texas – the question of human violence against animals is becoming increasingly important to us. This book is a result of years of reflection on our relationship to other species. We have arranged masses on animals' place in creation, held prayer services and lectured. Over coffee in church halls, fellow worshippers have challenged us: Haven't we been given animals for our use? Didn't Jesus eat meat? Such questions have forced us to ask if and how compassion for animals can be an embodiment of Christian faith. The book is also an answer to the question we have received from many of our friends in the peace movement: How can you focus on animals when so many humans are suffering?

We have also been inspired by our practical work in defense of animals. The hands-on experience of rescuing afflicted hens from factory farms has given us insight into Christ's continued suffering in the world.

Pelle performed some of his theological studies in jails and prisons, where he had been sentenced as a result of nonviolent activism on behalf of animals. To be locked in a cell can be a great environment for undisturbed thinking on important theological questions.

After years of work for nuclear disarmament and economic justice – including a stint as an inmate in an English prison – Annika became a deacon in the Church of Sweden. Before hundreds of attendees at her ordination, she promised "to stand on the side of the oppressed." Her work as a deacon – coordinating church outreach to poor people and refugees – has led her to ask what a commitment to justice means for the church's relationship to suffering animals.

We have lived and worked in many parts of the world, but our home country is Sweden and *Every Creature a Word of God: Compassion for Animals as Christian Spirituality* is a revised and expanded version of a book originally published in Swedish. We have tried to write a book that draws upon Christian experiences from different continents, languages and times. We both belong to a Lutheran church, but an ecumenical perspective is a matter of course for us, and we have been inspired by the richness of other spiritual traditions.

* * *

The term "spirituality" has grown popular in contemporary, western Christianity, yet there is no commonly accepted definition. It is often understood to relate to the inner life of a Christian: prayer, Bible reflection, meditation and fasting. In a broader sense, it can also mean the whole of Christian *life*. How do we lead our lives? What are we energized by? What are our commitments? Spirituality is about life and energy. This understanding draws from the root word "spirit." The Nicene Creed – written in the year 381 – calls the Holy Spirit "Giver of Life."

Spirituality has often been seen as an upwards exercise: that is, moving away from earthly constraints toward a transcendent experience of God. But in Christian spirituality, the direction should be the opposite. Our journey toward the divine mystery is downward. Some Christians have literally stooped over – like when Francis of Assisi bent to pick up worms on the road and move them to safety. Of course, it's mostly a metaphor to say that the direction of the Christian spiritual journey is downward. What we mean is that rather than sending our souls soaring to heaven, we should direct ourselves toward the earth: toward ourselves, toward our everyday life, toward creatures of flesh and blood.

Every creature is a word of God. Monks, mystics and teachers throughout church history echo this truth.[2] Every creature is an address from God: a word, a question to which we can reply with love.

The police disappeared into the distance, and the tension slowly dissolved. They probably weren't looking for us.

Our journey continued. After a couple of hours, the sun rose and shone level with the road. The unmistakably pungent smell of hens filled the car and from the trunk soft clucking noises could be heard.

Just hours ago, the hens had been crowded into small, steel cages. Soon they would be able to take their first steps in the grass, scratch the earth, stretch their wings, and feel the warmth of the sun on their feathers. Seventeen hens were about to start a new life.

– 1 –

PROCLAIM THE GOOD NEWS
TO CREATION

ANNIKA REMEMBERS: *I was nervous. Even though I was sure that I wanted to do this, it felt unpleasant. It was dark. People were sleeping in the houses around us and I had a crowbar in my hand. I had never opened a door with a crowbar. Luckily, my friend Rønnaug seemed calm. We left the car and walked toward the shed. It must be well insulated, we said to each other, because we couldn't hear any sounds from the hens inside.*

With some effort we worked the door open and Rønnaug walked in, opened one of the cages, and started to lift the hens out and place them in the cardboard boxes that we had brought with us. The hens flapped their wings. They were probably frightened even though we handled them carefully. I made sure that they didn't hop out of the boxes. Then we carried them, four hens to a box, out to the car. When they had all been loaded into the trunk, I pulled out the potted plant – a gift to the owner of the farm – and a letter explaining our action. I placed them both in a visible location near the empty cages. The letter included our names and telephone numbers.

John Woolman (1720–72) had a heart for the oppressed. The influential American Quaker and preacher would wander the countryside to demand better working conditions for poor laborers and to exhort slave owners to free their slaves. His compassion also extended to animals. Whoever lives in God's love, Woolman insisted, would feel tenderness toward all creatures. During a visit to England he refused to travel by stagecoach because the horses that pulled them were cruelly exploited, and often died of exhaustion. Rather than support such brutality, Woolman walked.

At the age of forty-nine, Woolman came down with pleurisy. His tongue became dry and his feet cold. The cold spread along his legs and up his body. "I was brought so near the gates of death that I forgot my name," he later wrote. He heard angels proclaim with "soft, melodious voices" that "John Woolman is dead":

> *I was then carried in spirit to the mines where poor oppressed people were digging rich treasures for those called Christians, and heard them blaspheme the name of Christ, at which I was grieved, for his name to me was precious. I was then informed that these heathens were told that those who oppressed them were the followers of Christ, and they said among themselves, "If Christ directed them to use us in this sort, then Christ is a cruel tyrant."[3]*

Woolman's vision is worth considering in context of our relationship with animals. The miners assumed – quite rationally – that the Christian god was evil, since the Christian mine owners were so abusive. The power that we humans hold over other species is even greater than that of the mine owners over their workers. We imprison animals, force-feed them, load them onto trucks bound for slaughter and kill them. They have no chance to defend themselves. If we use our power in this way, what does this say about us and our God? One contemporary animal advocate asks the question this way: "If angels imprisoned, tormented, and killed us the way we imprison, torment, and kill animals, would we believe that their treatment of us reflected the nature of a loving God? Would we consider them angels or demons?"[4]

We should try to reflect God's nature in our dealings with others, particularly when we are in a position of power. This ties in with the Bible's account of the earth's creation. As you will see in a later chapter, a common interpretation of that story is that God asks human beings to relate to animals in the same way that God relates to us: with nurturing and protective care.[5]

5

Reflecting God's Love

At the end of Mark's gospel, Jesus commands his disciples to "go into all the world and proclaim the good news to the whole creation."[6] All are loved by God. This should be proclaimed not only to humans, but to all of creation, since God's love surrounds all beings. Scripture reminds us that it is the nature of God to "love everything that exists."[7]

Many Christians have suggested that the good news should primarily be preached through action, rather than words. When it comes to animals, no other language can be used. It doesn't help them to hear us talk about God's love. So what does it mean then to preach the good news to animals? We're clear about what it cannot mean. We can't preach God's love to animals by hurting them. No, we testify to God's love for animals by showing them care and respect.

Saint Bartholomew lived in a small hermitage on the English island of Farne in the twelfth century. As he was sitting outside one day, he felt something pulling at the hem of his cloak. Looking down, he saw a mother eider frantically trying to catch his attention. She urged him along to a cleft in a nearby rock. On closer look, Bartholomew saw that one of the eider's ducklings had fallen into the crevice and was trapped. He climbed down and gently lifted the duckling to safety. The eider family took to the water, and Bartholomew went back to his hermitage – as the legend goes – "dumb with astonishment."[8]

Bartholomew's compassion and humility stand in sharp contrast to the heartlessness of the mine owners in John Woolman's vision, and serve as an example for all Christians who wish to live in a way that reflects God's love.

It's not easy to live a life with concern for the oppressed and vulnerable. We will fail again and again. But each attempt bears witness to the kind of God we profess.

– 2 –
THE WAY OF SERVICE

WE TEND TO THINK THAT GREATNESS means power over others, but Jesus had a radically different idea. "The greatest among you must become like the youngest," he said, "and the leader like one who serves."[9] Jesus directed this teaching to his closest disciples – those who held or wanted to hold leadership positions in the new Christian community. The established social order of Jesus' day – with those at the bottom of society serving those at the top – was turned on its head.

At the end of the gospel of John we find one illustration of this new, subversive order put into action. Using this story as a lens, a Christian social framework based in service becomes clear, and should have consequences for how we treat animals.

> *After he had washed their feet, had put on his robe, and had returned to the table, he said to them, "Do you know what I have done to you? You call me Teacher and Lord – and you are right, for that is what I am. So if I, your Lord and Teacher, have washed your feet, you also ought to wash one another's feet. For I have set you an example, that you also should do as I have done to you.*[10]

Some cultural context can help us understand just how remarkable it was for Jesus to wash his disciples' feet. Biblical scholar Luise Schotroff explains that within the strict division of labor practiced in Jesus' time, only women and slaves (usually female slaves) performed the task of foot washing. In other words, those at the very bottom of the social order washed the feet of those at the top. Jesus overturned this hierarchy of gender and social class when he – a free man – washed the feet of his disciples, included among them women. It was unheard of for a teacher to wash the feet of his followers. Yet this was the kind of power that Jesus wanted his disciples to practice.

"Power shall no longer be power from up to down," writes Schotroff. "Power exists only where it emanates out of the relationship to God and Jesus. And this presupposes a clear step: to refrain from dominion, in the sense of the hierarchies' meaning."[11]

Abuse of Power

Another hierarchical order exists today: our tyrannical dominion over animals. We need conversion from this order to new ways of living.

Most Christians think that animals should be treated humanely. But isn't it going too far to talk about serving them? After all, humankind is the pinnacle of creation! Serving animals, we might protest, would be to lower ourselves to a level where we do not belong.

But what is God's revelation in Christ? God "lowered" himself to the level of creation. As Paul writes in his letter to the Philippians: "[Christ Jesus], though he was in the form of God, did not regard equality with God as something to be exploited, but emptied himself, taking the form of a slave, being born in human likeness."[12]

We're called to serve, yet we continue to exploit. It's difficult to resist the corrupting influence of power. It's difficult to support social change when our ego is propped up by the status quo. It was in the selfish interests of free men that female slaves were at hand to wash them, but Jesus challenged this custom.

Many people today feel that it is in their interests that hot dogs and steak are available in the grocery store.[13] As Christians, we should ask ourselves if this is a responsible exercise of power.

Lessons from Church History

The spirit of Jesus calls us to a relationship with other creatures that is characterized by service and care-giving. Throughout the history of the church, many people have applied this evangelical attitude. For example, Saint Jerome (347–420) and his monks washed the feet of tired camels and other animals that found refuge at their monastery in Bethlehem.[14]

Saint Francis of Assisi (1182–1226) praised holy obedience to God as a measure to control selfishness. "Obedience subjects a man to everyone on earth," he said. "And not only to men, but to all the beasts as well and to the wild animals."[15] Francis is reported to have built nests for turtle doves and supplied bees with honey and wine during the winter to protect them from dying in the cold.

Saint Columba (521–97) once pulled aside one of the monks at his monastery on the Scottish island of Iona. He told the young man to travel to the west side of the island and keep watch from the rocks above the shoreline. "A guest will arrive from the north of Ireland," he said, "a heron, buffeted by the wind on her long flight, tired and weary. Her strength will be almost gone and she will fall on the shore in front of you. Take care how you lift her up, having pity for her, and carry her to the nearby house. Look after her and feed her there as a guest for three days and nights. Afterwards, at the end of three days, when the heron is revived, she will no longer want to stay as a pilgrim with us, but when her strength is recovered she will return to the sweet districts of Ireland from which she came."

The monk obeyed. He waited at the shoreline and, as Columba had foretold, the heron arrived and collapsed upon reaching land. He lifted her from the shore and carried her to the house. She was hungry and he offered her food. After three days, the heron had regained her strength and flew home.[16]

In many ways our societies are more egalitarian today than in Jesus' time. The labor, civil rights and women's movements, among others, have helped us to correct some of the power imbalances between people. In our relationship to animals, however, this imbalance is intact – and it couldn't be any other way. We have power over the rest of creation and cannot evade our responsibility. But how should this power be exercised? To exploit the powerless is not consistent with the values embodied by Jesus.

– 3 –

AND GOD MADE
THE VEGETARIAN

ANNIKA REMEMBERS: *It was still early when we arrived. The house stood to our left on a grassy slope, and the porch light had been left on. To our right was a hen house with a fenced-in yard. All was quiet when I approached the hen house and peeked inside. Maybe the five hens that were already there were still sleeping. We brought in the first box and slowly opened it. We lifted the freed hens out of the box and set them in the hay. They took small steps and looked around at their new home. It was lovely to see them.*

The owner of the farm came down the hill from the house, sleepy but smiling. She said that in a couple of days she would let the new hens walk outside in the yard. A few weeks later I called to ask how the hens were adjusting. "Wonderfully," she answered.

The word "myth" is used in everyday speech to mean a misconception or untruth. But it also describes a certain kind of story. Myths talk about the most fundamental questions of life, helping us interpret our existence and find new ways of living. They should not be read as scientific accounts of past events. But that doesn't make them unimportant. They function to throw the reader straight into burning existential and moral questions.

The first pages of the Bible describe the creation of the earth. It's one of the most widely read myths in Western literature. From our point of view, the theological and moral questions this story raises are fascinating. The people who transcribed the story lived in a society that was permeated by the use of animals. They depended on animals for – among other things – food, clothing, tents, wineskins and tools.[17] In this context, it would have been natural for the writers to legitimize their lifestyle, perhaps by letting God say: "I give you all the animals. They will be yours for food." But instead they described an idyllic garden in which humans and animals live in peace, and people eat plants. God says to the first humans: "I give you every seed-bearing plant on the face of the whole earth, and every tree that has fruit with seed in it. They will be yours for food."[18] The diet in Eden might have included grains, seeds, apricots, olives, figs, dates, pomegranates, nuts, blackberries, and grapes.[19] In the beginning, God created the vegetarian.

If we want to imitate life in paradise, wrote Gregory of Nyssa (330–395), we should avoid meat and instead live on "fruit, cereals and vegetables."[20] He was one of several early church writers to lift up the spiritual benefits of plant-based food. In the eastern Orthodox churches, this tradition lives on in the discipline of fasting. During the long fast before Easter, observant Egyptians, Russians and Greeks refrain from meat and other animal foods in accordance with Adam and Eve's diet.[21] Egyptian Coptic priest Tadros Y. Malaty writes: "It is noteworthy to underline that the first man was vegetarian (Gen. 1:29), and man continued to avoid eating meat until the period of Noah's ark (Gen. 9:3). At this time his spiritual standard dropped. This explains why believers eat vegetarian food when they wish to create a suitable atmosphere for spiritual development."[22]

In the western churches, the picture is different. Only a minority of believers have made an issue of the diet practiced in Paradise (members of the nineteenth-century Bible Christian Church, and the eighteenth century Quaker preacher Joshua Evans, for example). Most people don't even notice it. In his book *Good Eating*, theologian Stephen Webb writes about giving a presentation to a Christian adult education forum. During the presentation he pointed out to the audience that Adam and Eve were vegetarians. The minister of the church was taken aback and insisted that Webb must be mistaken.[23]

We have been writing about the creation story in the singular, but in fact the Bible offers two different accounts. We focus on the first in this chapter, but note that in the second account God also gives people a plant-based diet, placing them in a garden surrounded by fruit trees.[24]

Like a Righteous King

Humankind's relationship to animals is an important theme in both creation accounts. The first describes humankind as the image of God, made to rule over animals:

> *Then God said, "let us make man in our image, in our like-ness, and let them* rule *over the fish of the sea and the birds of the air, over the livestock, over all the earth, and over the creatures that move along the ground." So God created man in his own* image, *in the* image *of God he created him; male and female he created them. God blessed them and said to them, "be fruitful and increase in number; fill the earth and subdue it.* Rule *over the fish of the sea and the birds of the air and over every living creature that moves on the ground."*[25] *[emphasis added]*

Translators usually render the Hebrew word radah as "rule" in English. It sounds strong, and might provoke images of brutal tyrants, of ancient kings who oppressed their people. But the Biblical authors didn't have a despot in mind when they wrote about humankind as ruler of creation. The text weaves together the two characteristics of the ideal ruler: one who is righteous in his decisions and one who has a particular responsibility to the vulnerable. The Psalms describe a good king this way:

> *For he will deliver the needy who cry out,*
> *the afflicted who have no-one to help.*
> *He will take pity on the weak and the needy*
> *and save the needy from death.*
> *He will rescue them from oppression and violence,*
> *for precious is their blood in his sight.*[26]

Old Testament scholar Gordon Wenham writes that God commissions humanity "to rule nature as benevolent king, acting as God's representative over them and therefore treating them in the same way as God who created them."[27] Before him, in 1728, the Scottish poet James Thomson wrote that humanity is "The Lord and not the Tyrant of the world."[28] In 1748, the philosopher and theologian David Hartley reflected on humankind's relationship to animals: "We seem to be in the place of God to them and we are obliged by the same tenure to be their guardians and benefactors."[29]

Directly after they are told to rule over creation, the first humans get their instructions to eat a plant-based diet. One idea is naturally connected to the other. The righteous ruler cares for his subjects. He doesn't kill and eat them.

Today, many people see creation from a self-serving perspective, assuming that animals were created for our unrestricted use. But the Genesis stories turn this perspective on its head. Animals were not created for us to exploit. Rather, we were created to guard and protect them.

God's Concession

On the sixth day, "God saw all that he had made, and it was very good."[30] But peace doesn't last long. Sin sweeps over the earth like a plague. God decides to let a flood wash the earth clean. Only Noah's family and the animals on board the ark survive. When the water recedes, God says to Noah and his sons that "everything that lives and moves will be food for you. Just as I gave you the green plants, I now give you everything. But you must not eat meat that has its lifeblood still in it."[31]

By its greed and violence, humankind has destroyed the old order. God concedes that humans are incapable of living in peace with other creatures, and offers a compromise: Animals may be eaten, but not their blood. Blood is a symbol of life, and this prohibition is a reminder that all life belongs to God.[32]

It might be strange to think of God making concessions to human weakness. But this isn't the only example in the Bible. In the first book of Samuel, for instance, the Israelites ask God to give them a king so they can be like the other nations. God warns them about the dangers of this kind of social order, but the people insist. God finally relents and gives them a king.[33]

Jesus argued that men should not be allowed to divorce their wives. Some people disagreed and pointed out that they clearly have this right under the law given to them by God through Moses. To this Jesus replied, "it was because you were so hard-hearted that Moses allowed you to divorce your wives, but from the beginning it was not so."[34] If we were to apply Jesus' reasoning to the question of diet, we could say that it was because of our heard-heartedness that God allowed us to eat animals. "But from the beginning it was not so."

As Bible readers, we are confronted with a decision: Is our moral starting point found in God's compromise with Noah or in God's original plan? The concession or the ideal?

Jesus Among Leopards

Several Biblical texts repeat the theme of peace between humans and animals. The prophet Isaiah foresaw a time when creation's good order is reestablished.

> The wolf will live with the lamb,
> the leopard will lie down with the goat,
> the calf and the lion and the yearling together;
> and a little child will lead them.
> The cow will feed with the bear,
> their young will lie down together,
> and the lion will eat straw like the ox.
> The infant will play near the hole of the cobra,
> and the young child put his hand into the viper's nest.
> They will neither harm nor destroy on all my holy mountain,
> For the earth will be full of the knowledge of the Lord
> as the waters cover the sea.[35]

This theme reemerges early in Mark's gospel when Jesus went out into the wilderness "and he was with the wild beasts." The Greek words that are translated "he was with" are often used in the New Testament in a positive sense to express close association, friendship or agreement.[36] Which animals Mark had in mind we don't know – perhaps leopards, antelopes, foxes, scorpions, or wild donkeys. The important point is that Jesus lived in harmony with the animals he encountered. Jesus' journey to the wilderness reminds the reader of God's intentions for a peaceful creation.[37]

The fourth century monk Theon had a great affinity with the animals of the Egyptian desert. "The tracks of gazelle and goat and the wild ass were thick about his cell," reads a story that was popular in the early church. "They said of him that at night he would go out to the desert, and for company a great troop of the beasts of the desert would go with him. And he would draw water from his well and offer them cups of it."[38]

Maybe Jesus' journey to the wilderness inspired Theon and the other hermits that lived among animals. But in our contemporary urban churches, this story is largely forgotten. Remembering Jesus' encounter with the animals would surely add to our understanding of him as a man of peace and reconciliation.

Creation's Sabbath

On the sixth day, God made all creatures that walk on land, the beasts of the earth and humans. On the seventh day God rested. The day of rest is the completion and crown of creation. God blesses the Sabbath day and makes it holy. Humans, sheep, cows, donkeys – all creatures have the right to a full day of rest on the Sabbath. In one of Saint Bridget of Sweden's (1303–73) visions, God talked about the connection between the Sabbath and care for animals. "Let a man fear, above all, me, his God, and so much the gentler will he become towards my creatures and animals, in whom, on account of me, their creator, he ought to have compassion; for to that end was rest ordained on the Sabbath."[39]

As rulers of creation, we humans have been given the responsibility to administer the care and rest that God desires for all creatures.

ANNIKA REMEMBERS: *In the photograph I'm standing at the far left, smiling wearily. We'd been awake all night. Now at five o'clock the next day we were standing in front of the large supermarket* Konsum *with a banner saying* KONSUM WITHOUT BATTERY-CAGE EGGS. *Sometimes a passerby would take a leaflet, which explained why we had rescued the hens and why we wanted to see grocery stores without battery-cage eggs. A crew from the regional TV station had just interviewed us, and the news segment later that evening was positive.*

Before our demonstration, a representative of the supermarket chain had explained to us in an email that they couldn't stop selling eggs from hens in cages; they didn't have enough free-range suppliers to keep up with the demand. But there we stood in the afternoon sun.

A few months later I saw a large ad at a trolley stop announcing that Konsum *would no longer sell battery-cage eggs.*

WHO IS
MY NEIGHBOR?

PELLE REMEMBERS: *Winter 1999. The golf course appears on our left, marking that we're almost there.*

"And if we're caught?"

"We don't need to apologize for anything," says Helena. "We have nothing to be ashamed of."

"I still feel uneasy," I say.

"You can think of the hens," she says, "of what their lives are like."

We park behind a barn and she walks across the muddy yard, straight toward the shed with the hens.

I stand there motionless in the field of vision of the farmer's kitchen window.

Doing recon in the middle of the day, whose idea was that?

She disappears in through the door of the shed, leaving me alone, but returns after a few seconds.

"Oh yes, there are cages," she says.

Locks? Doors?

"Unlocked," she says.

The farmer comes out of the house in rubber boots. He walks resolutely down the hill towards us.

"Were you inside?" he asks at a few yards' distance, "were you inside?"

I mumble something as I stretch out my hand to greet him.

"We are examining the possibility of liberating hens," says Helena.

The farmer's wife and son join him. The son is perhaps six or seven years old and is standing in front of his mother. He leans back into her, and she puts her arms around him. They stand together.

"You're surely not going to steal from us."

"We can't promise that," answers Helena.

They had seen on TV a story about hens being liberated from another farm in the same region.

"Was that you?" asks the man.

"No," says Helena, "but we plan to do something similar."

He says that that would surely be considered breaking and entering and that someone might be shot for it. No one reacts to his threat.

And what did they think about the other action they had seen on TV?

He laughs under his breath. "Well," he says, "some people thought it was cute."

"One tries to take care of the hens as well as one can," says the wife.

"Those six hens got a new home," I say. "What do you think about that, seen from the hens' perspective?"

A short silence.

"It was probably best for the hens," she says quietly.

She says again, "It was probably best."

"You shall love your neighbor," said Jesus.

"And who is my neighbor?" a lawyer asked.

Jesus replied: "A man was going down from Jerusalem to Jericho, and fell into the hands of robbers, who stripped him, beat him, and went away, leaving him half dead. Now by chance a priest was going down that road; and when he saw him, he passed by on the other side. So likewise a Levite, when he came to the place and saw him, passed by on the other side. But a Samaritan while traveling came near him; and when he saw him he was moved with pity. He went to him and bandaged his wounds, having poured oil and wine on them. Then he put him on his own animal, brought him to an inn and took care of him. The next day he took out two denarii, gave them to the innkeeper, and said, 'take care of him; and when I come back, I will repay you whatever more you spend.' Which of these three, do you think, was a neighbor to the man who fell into the hands of the robbers?"

He said, "the one who showed him mercy."

Jesus said to him, "go and do likewise." [40]

Love can mean many different things. In modern western culture, romantic love stands in the center. But Jesus lifts up another form of love: compassion that leads to action. This kind of love asks us to tend to the needs of others, even at a personal sacrifice.

Jesus' parable must be understood against the backdrop of a deep cultural conflict between Jews and Samaritans. The story is not only about the hands-on nature of love, but also about love's ability to overcome divisions. When a Samaritan took on responsibility for caring for a Jew, he broke with existing social norms. When Jesus elevated a Samaritan as a moral example, he astounded his Jewish audience.

What is unique about Jesus, writes the Lutheran Archbishop KG Hammar, is "his unwillingness or even incapacity to create borders since God's love knows no borders." To follow Jesus, we too must practice a love that overcomes division. Building walls of separation between ourselves and others, Hammar reminds us, is an expression of our incapacity to love.

Where then does this border-crossing love take us? Many people extend their love beyond the species border by living with and caring for dogs and cats. But with other animals we tend to fortify our walls of separation. Each year billions of farm animals are raised for food – more than 10 billion in the US alone. Few of us would say that we simply don't care about cows and chickens. But when we (like the priest and the Levite) turn from their plight, we witness to our incapacity to love.[41]

Reverence for Life

Albert Schweitzer (1875—1965) grew up in a devout religious home in a small community on the border of France and Germany. "Even before I went to school," he wrote in his memoirs, "it seemed incomprehensible to me why I in my evening prayers should only pray for humans. Therefore, when my mother kissed me goodnight and left the room, I secretly added a prayer that I had composed myself for all living creatures. It ran like this: Heavenly father, watch over and bless all things that breathe; protect them from all evil, and let them sleep in peace."[42]

As an adult, Schweitzer became a well-respected scholar and musician. But he left this life behind in order to work as a doctor in present-day Gabon, on Africa's west coast.

At his clinic, no-one was turned away, regardless of religion or skin color. Animals that were brought to the clinic were also provided the best possible medical care. Schweitzer was impatient with the lack of interest that western intellectuals had shown in animals. "Just like the housewife who has scrubbed the house carefully, shut the door to prevent any dog from coming in and spoiling her work with the marks of his paws, so have religious and philosophical thinkers remained vigilant against animals running around in their ethical theories. The stupidities they are guilty of, in order to uphold traditional narrow-heartedness and raise it to principle, borders on the incredible. They have either entirely dismissed all sympathy for animals, or they have taken pains to diminish it to almost nothing."[43]

During his work in Africa, Schweitzer sought after a new ethic that could lead humanity into the future. It came to him during a trip on the Ogowé River. The barge that he sat on was pulled slowly upstream by a tugboat. He tried to take notes, but wasn't able to concentrate his thoughts. He felt disheartened and tired. On the third day, he passed a small island in the middle of the wide river. It was dusk; the sun was setting over the jungle. Along a sandbank, four hippopotami walked with their young. The words suddenly came to him: "Reverence for life." He had never before read nor heard this expression.

The core of Schweitzer's ethical vision was this: "I am life that wants to live, in the midst of life that wants to live." It's good to preserve and promote life. It's evil to destroy and injure life.

In 1952, Schweitzer received the Nobel Peace Prize. In his acceptance speech at the University of Oslo, he said that ethics has its roots in compassion, which "can only attain its full breadth and depth if it embraces all living creatures and does not limit itself to mankind."[44]

The Fatal Dividing Line

Jesus often broke with the values of his time. He tried to erase the lines that divided rich and poor, clean and unclean, righteous and sinners. He embraced children, even though they were considered insignificant. In one gospel story, however, Jesus defends the kind of us-and-them thinking that he otherwise worked against.

In this story, a woman begs Jesus to cure her daughter. She is an outsider: a Canaanite. Jesus answers her plea with prejudice and cold-heartedness: "It is not fair to take the children's food and throw it to the dogs." ("Children" refers to Jewish people, while "dog" was a condescending term for non-Jews.) The woman persists. She argues with Jesus until he gives in and cures her daughter.[45]

Archbishop Hammar thinks that this scene in Matthew's gospel reflects the difficult religious questions facing the early church. Was Jesus directing his life and message exclusively to the Jewish community, or was his message relevant also to non-Jews? "You can almost hear the stormy debates in the Matthean community," writes Hammar. "Should the borders be crossed, even the religious, even the ones that could be drawn with the support of Scripture, with the support of tradition? Didn't the examples that were constantly retold from the life of Jesus show that he always crossed borders if love were at stake?"[46]

Much has changed since Jesus' time. Many of the walls that he tried to pull down have now fallen. But there are still borders that are upheld and patrolled. One of the most striking and well-guarded is the border between us and other species. This division has dramatic consequences: it justifies a worldview in which other beings can be locked into concrete buildings, 24 hours a day, and then killed for food.

When someone tries to establish a border with such fatal consequences, our task as Christians is – like the Canaanite woman – to persistently claim the overflowing love that wants life and health for everyone, humans and animals alike.

21

– 5 –
THAT OF GOD IN EVERY BEING:
CREATION AS SACRAMENT

ANNIKA REMEMBERS: *When I got off the bus and looked up at the kitchen window, he was always sitting there at the table looking at me. I used to think about how long he had sat there, if he somehow could feel that I or my sister were on our way home. Every time I opened the door he showed the same enthusiasm: he jumped up at me and ran back and forth across the living room. His tail wagged quickly. I lay down on the floor, cuddled with him, and he licked my face. There were no reproaches for having left him alone in the house for several hours. Just sheer happiness about my return.*

"Love animals, love plants, love each thing," preaches the Russian monk Zosima in Fyodor Dostoevsky's novel *The Brothers Karamazov.* "If you love each thing, you will perceive the mystery of God in things. Once you have perceived it, you will begin tirelessly to perceive more and more of it every day. And you will come at last to love the whole world with an entire, universal love. Love the animals: God gave them the rudiments of thought and an untroubled joy. Do not trouble it, do not torment them, do not take their joy from them, do not go against God's purpose."[47]

Animals carry secrets that we humans are often unable to see. Whoever loves animals will discover that God has a purpose for them outside of their usefulness to humans. Zosima's sermon places us in front of a challenging question: are we mature enough to accept that God interacts with other creatures; that we are not the only beloved child; that we have brothers and sisters?

"The mystery of God in things" comes through in a true story from the book *Animal Grace* by psychologist Mary Lou Randour. A woman takes a break from her hike along the coast of northern California. She stretches out and relaxes on a large rock jutting out over the ocean. As she listens to the waves, the hair on the back of her neck stands on end. Someone is watching her. She pulls herself up and sees a whale resting on the water.

Their eyes meet. The woman experiences eternal stillness. Categories such as 'them' and 'us' are dissolved; she feels herself "flow into a seamless web of existence, in which all of life is one." For Randour, this event illustrates how exceptional encounters across the species border can be. Since we cannot identify ourselves with animals in the same way as with other humans, animals force us to transcend our limited human perspectives. To open ourselves to that which is different is an exercise in spirituality. "How can we come to know God, or grasp the interconnectedness of all life, if we limit ourselves to knowing only our own kind?"[48]

Animals as Icons

The word "sacrament" generally means a specific religious rite that expresses our relationship with God. Most Christians consider baptism and Eucharist to be sacraments. But the word can also be used in a wider sense. "Sacramentalism" means being open to see God's presence in all of creation – a world which bears witness to the diversity and inexhaustible richness of the Divine.[49] Every created being is an icon (from the Greek word for image), writes Catholic theologian James Gaffney, and "the more intricate and exquisite are material creatures, the more transparent are they to the glory of their Creator." In this view, our relationship to animals becomes a spiritual issue. Not only should Christians be filled with care and compassion for them; animals should be the object of "awe and devotion."[50]

The work of Francis Jammes (1868–1938) – a poet and devout Catholic from the small border town of Orthez, France – is infused with this sacramental view of the world. "There is in the look of beasts a profound light and gentle sorrow," he wrote in 1903, "which fills me with such understanding that my soul opens like a hospice to all the sorrows of animals.

"They are forever in my heart, as when I see a tired horse, his nose drooping to the ground, asleep in the nocturnal rain, before a café; or the agony of a cat crushed beneath a carriage; or a wounded sparrow who has found refuge in a hole in a wall. Were it not for the feeling that it is undignified for a man, I would kneel before such patience and such torments, for I seem to see a halo around the heads of these mournful creatures, a real halo, as large as the universe, placed there by God Himself."[51]

The Mystical Discovery

There's a growing interest in the Christian mystical tradition, even among previously skeptical Protestant audiences. This isn't necessarily good if it means that we are only seeking spiritual *experiences*, in self-serving explorations of the "inner chambers of the soul." But authentic mysticism is never an escape from the world, writes the Dutch Catholic theologian Edward Schillebeeckx. The mystical experience is a breakthrough, a collapse of the old world, an experience of something entirely new. Out of this grows a "conciliatory compassion with all. Approach, not flight."[52]

One characteristic of Christian mysticism is that the relationship with God is experienced as a fusion: human and God are united. Rather than falling on their knees in front of a heavenly king, mystics seek to sink into and be engulfed in God's love. Whoever lives in this kind of intimacy with God sees God's face in unexpected places. The mystic has an unusual capacity to recognize God in all of creation. All living beings are pulled into the mystic's awe-inspiring discovery: we are all inseparably united with one another.[53] The journey into the Divine Mystery becomes, by definition, a journey toward the creatures of the world. Close association, compassion, identification: these are key concepts in the mystical vision. They are well summarized by Francis Jammes:

"Yesterday I was at a fair, and watched the merry-go-round. There was an ass among the wooden animals. The sight of it almost made me weep, because I was reminded of those living martyrs, its brothers.

"I wanted to pray, and to say to it: Little ass, you are my brother. They say that you are stupid, because you are incapable of doing evil. You go your slow pace, and seem to think as you walk: 'See! I cannot go any faster...The poor make use of me, because they need not give me much to eat.' Little ass, the goad pricks you. Then you go a little faster, but not a great deal. You cannot go very fast...Sometimes you fall. Then they beat you, and pull at the rein fastened to the bit in your mouth. They pull so hard that your lips are drawn back showing your poor, yellow teeth which browse on miseries."[54]

Identification and compassion do not exclude prophetic criticism. On the contrary, they work hand-in-hand. "Ah!" Jammes laments at the sight of animal cruelty, "what a prostitution of God's creatures."

Humility

The environmental and animal rights movements often share common concerns. When forests are clear cut and waterways poisoned, for instance, animal habitat is destroyed. But animals and nature should not be reflexively lumped together. There is a difference between kicking a stone and doing the same to a field mouse. Without belittling the spiritual experience that nature provides, it's important to see that the human-animal relationship has a particular dynamic and richness. It can become an encounter between an "I" and a "Thou," in which something of God can be revealed.[55] John Woolman wrote in his *Journal* that "true religion" means not only love of God, but also a commitment to justice and goodness for all inhabitants of the earth. In them the face of God is revealed. "[A]s the mind was moved by an inward principle to love God as an invisible, incomprehensible Being, so, by the same principle, it was moved to love him in all his manifestations in the visible world; that, as by his breath the flame of life was kindled in all animal sensible creatures, to say we love God as unseen, and at the same time exercise cruelty toward the least creature moving by his life, or by life derived from him, was a contradiction in itself."[56]

Quakers speak of "that of God in every person." This outlook seems to have influenced their way of relating to human beings. They are often on the front lines of social movements, from the abolition of slavery to prison reform. The Quakers are one of few denominations to reaffirm the pacifism of the early church. Seeing "God in every person" is a good reason not to kill.

Inspired by Woolman, we could also talk about "that of God in every creature," and accordingly approach animals with curiosity and humility – not hurting and killing them. "I felt very close to God or felt religious awe anyway," wrote Thomas Merton, after encountering a flock of warblers. "Watching those birds was a food for meditation or a mystical reading. Perhaps better."[57]

Animals as Spiritual Guides

People often degrade animals in order to justify their exploitation. But animal advocates also run the risk of belittling animals by stressing their powerlessness. We often forget that most wild animals can do perfectly well without our assistance. All they require of us is that we stop oppressing them and destroying their habitat. Animals are not only recipients of our benevolence. They are also agents.

The tsunami was fast approaching the Indian south coast on December 26, 2004. A woman named Sangeeta carried her two youngest children up a nearby mountain to safety. Her eldest boy didn't follow. As Sangeeta panicked, Selvakumar, the family dog, went after the boy. He found him hiding in the family's house, near the seashore. Selvakumar grabbed the collar of the boy's shirt, pulled him out of the house and led him up the mountain just in time to escape the colossal waves. "That dog is my God," said Sangeeta a week after the incident. At her side lay Selvakumar, sleeping on the warm asphalt.[58]

Animals can save people in other ways. In his book *Unnatural Order*, Jim Mason shares several stories of animals being agents of healing for severely traumatized people. One case involved an autistic six year old girl who had never spoken to anyone and recoiled at human touch. But when a dove was brought into her nursery and took to flight, something amazing happened. One psychiatrist writes that her face lost "the withdrawn, inward, immobile expression of a severely disturbed child" and she became "an apparently normal girl radiating joy."[59]

And animals can serve as teachers. "He enjoys simple pleasures and takes each day as it comes" writes Unitarian Universalist minister Gary Kowalski about his dog, Chinook. "Like a true Zen master, he eats when he's hungry and sleeps when he's tired. He's not hung up about sex. Best of all, he befriends me with an unconditional love that human beings would do well to emulate ... When I become too serious and preoccupied, he reminds me of the importance of frolicking and play. When I get too wrapped up in abstractions and ideas, he reminds me of the importance of exercising and caring for my body. On his own canine level, he shows me that it might be possible to live without inner conflicts or neuroses: uncomplicated, genuine, and glad to be alive."[60]

Many hundreds of years earlier, Job was having a hearty theological debate with some of his friends. If they want proof that all of creation is in God's hands, he tells his friends, "ask the animals, and they will teach you, or the birds of the air, and they will tell you."[61] The idea that animals can serve as teachers has been repeated many times throughout the history of the church.[62] "A dog is better than I am," said the early desert monk Abba Xanthios, "for he has love and he does not judge."[63]

Relationships are about reciprocity. We can't expect only to change the other, but must also be open to change ourselves. To be a friend of animals means being ready to learn and receive from them.

PELLE REMEMBERS: *The usual. Rows of steel cages stacked on top of each other, and the sound of thousands of wings beating against metal. But in the light of our headlamps, something unexpected appeared: a lone hen scampered across the concrete corridor that ran between the wall and a row of cages. She could not have been free for long – maybe an hour, since the owner was last there. But how did she escape?*

Helena approached the hen. "I knew that if I was going to catch her, I'd need to be quick," she told us afterwards. The hen was bouncing across the floor. Helena stooped over and outstretched her arms. With one quick step, she lunged forward and grasped the hen. This was the first hen we rescued that night, and we lifted her gently into one of the boxes. Twenty-three more to go.

We had to work at opening some of the cages, which were closed with steal wire. I grabbed hold of my first hen, and carefully pulled her out, afraid that her claws would get snagged on the mesh floor of the cage.

You could feel the warmth of the hens through the protective gloves, Helena reminisced a few days later.

Yes, and the feather shaft. And the light body.

− 6 −
MELANGELL AND THE HARE: THE EXAMPLE OF THE SAINTS

WHEN THE NEW TESTAMENT AUTHORS talk about "the saints," they don't mean people with particular spiritual resources. All believers belonged to the community of saints, and were expected to lead a holy life. Over time, "saint" became an honorary title given to people who led exemplary and morally upstanding lives. The church began to celebrate the day of their death. Chapels were built over their graves. The saints were thought to live close to God in heaven, and Christians began to ask them to intercede on their behalf.

Of course, the saints have always been highly regarded in the Roman Catholic and Orthodox Churches. Protestant reformers of the sixteenth century reacted to what they considered cults of saints. But they continued to lift up many of these saints as inspiring examples, that Christians might "follow their faith and good works."[64] All Saints Day is still celebrated in many churches born of the European Reformation, and testifies to the legacy of saints across the Christian world. No matter our background, then, reading about the saints can give us new perspectives on what it means to live a Christian life. In this chapter, we'll look more closely at some saints to see what they can teach us about right relationships between humans and animals.

According to Nathan Söderblom, a pioneering ecumenist and recipient of the 1930 Nobel Peace Prize, a saint is a person who "with all his being, in life and deed, shows that God is alive."[65] His definition does not, however, say anything about the nature of God. We would add that the saints show us *who* the living God is. They show us that God loves all of God's creatures. Such a confession is radical in a world where most animals are treated as if there is no God who loves them.

Common Origin

"Listen to the Word of God," said Anthony of Padua (1195-1231), standing at the seashore and preaching to an unusual congregation. "My brother fish, you have a great obligation, according to your ability, to give thanks to your Creator, who has given you such a noble element for your home. You have fresh or salt water, as you like. And he has given you many shelters to avoid storms."[66] Anthony is by no means the only saint to have regarded animals as his family. Saint Bonaventure (1221–74) wrote in his biography of Francis of Assissi that "he would call creatures, no matter how small, by the name of 'brother' or 'sister,' because he knew they shared with him the same beginning."[67] This kinship was likewise expressed by John Chrysostom (344–407): "Surely we ought to show kindness and gentleness to animals for many reasons, and chiefly because they are of the same origin as ourselves."[68] Humans and animals "had in the beginning almost the same origins," wrote the German mystic Hildegard of Bingen (1098-1179). In paradise, "animals and beasts intermingled with people and people with them, whence they loved each other greatly and unwontedly and were bound to each other."[69]

These saints remind us of the communion between animals and humans. We have a common origin and share a common home. We have the same creator, we were created on the same day from the same material ("the dust of the ground"),[70] we received the same blessing, and we rested on the same Sabbath. We were given the same plants to eat. Our destinies are intertwined; we were saved in the same ark and participate in the same covenant and promise.[71] According to the Hebrew prophets, we share the same future: the peaceable kingdom on God's holy mountain.

Friends of the Hunted

A Welsh prince and his hunting party were pursuing a hare when the animal slipped out of sight into a bramble patch. In the thicket they were surprised to find a woman praying, the hare "lying boldly and fearlessly" in the fold of her dress. This didn't stop the prince. He ordered his dogs to attack, but some sort of force kept them from getting near. They howled and retreated. The prince was amazed at what he saw, and concluded that God had protected the hare. He declared the entire valley a sanctuary for asylum-seekers. According to legend, the praying woman – Saint Melangell (d.590) – continued to live on this land for thirty-seven years, and "the hares, which are little wild creatures, surrounded her every day of her life, just as they had been tame or domesticated animals."[72]

Similar stories can be found about many of the saints.[73] Anselm of Canterbury (1033–1109) was traveling one day when a pack of hunting dogs chased a wild hare into the path. The frightened animal took refuge beneath Anselm's horse, which the saint ordered still. The dogs could not reach the hare, and the hunters laughed at the situation. But Anselm burst into tears. "You laugh, do you?" he cried. "But there is no laughing, no merry-making, for this unhappy beast." He ordered the dogs not to chase the animal. "Then the hare leapt up unhurt, and swiftly returned to its fields and woods," wrote Anselm's secretary Eadmer, "while we, no longer laughing and not a little uplifted by so affecting a deliverance for the frightened animal, followed the Father along our appointed way."[74]

The Psalmist exclaims, "you save humans and animals alike, O LORD."[75] The saints live out God's desire for all creatures to be safe from danger and oppression. The saints don't seek conflict, but neither do they withdraw from confrontation with those who wish to harm animals. This is the condition of brother- and sisterhood. If our brothers and sisters are threatened, we must intervene.

Fear of conflict is one reason why people do not choose to stand in defense of animals. In a society where meat-eating is the norm, even the humblest vegetarian may be viewed as an antagonist. At a family Christmas dinner, for instance, the notable absence of ham on one person's plate might be viewed as a critical commentary on everyone else. To be accommodating and contribute to a pleasant atmosphere are good character traits, but sometimes we need to stir the pot.

A person who clearly demonstrated this was Saint Godric (1069-1170). A former sea captain, Godric lived for many years as a hermit in the forest of Finchale, near Durham, England. There he composed songs, tended to his gardens, and welcomed pilgrims who came to him for spiritual guidance. Reginald of Durham, one of Godric's contemporaries, wrote that the saint would allow hares, mice and other animals into his hermitage during the cold winters. He even allowed snakes to warm themselves by his fire, asking only that they not disturb his prayers. During particularly harsh weather, Godric would look under thick hedges for animals that were cold or had lost their way. If he found any, he would pick them up and warm them against his chest.

Godric would often snatch captured animals out of the hands of hunters, releasing them back into the wild. The hunters responded by trying to hide their prey. But Godric knew where they were hidden. He would head straight to the hiding places, writes Reginald, "and while the man would stand by crimson with fear and confusion, he would lift them out and set them free."

Hunted animals often sought Godric's aid. On one occasion, an exhausted stag appeared outside his hermitage. The saint let the stag in and stood watch outside the door for its hunters. They soon arrived and asked Godric if he had seen the animal, to which Godric replied: "God knows where he may be."

Perhaps Godric's answer to the hunters was more than a clever way around violating the eighth commandment against lying. Perhaps it was a recognition that no being is ever forgotten by God. As Jesus explained, not a single sparrow falls to the ground without God knowing of it.[76] When the ravens' young cry out in hunger, God tells Job, I provide them with food.[77]

Another of Godric's biographers writes that for years following his rescue, the stag would visit his protector, lying at the saint's feet in gratitude.[78]

To Challenge the Status Quo

In his famous book published in 1516, Thomas More (the patron saint of politicians), introduces his readers to his vision of an ideally perfect society: *Utopia*. Utopia is characterized by social justice and enlightenment – a stark contrast to what he saw in his native England. More's Utopia is a comparatively egalitarian society that enjoyed free access to health care and education, as well as something that would be radical even for our time: a six hour work day.

More has been considered one of the pioneers of the socialist philosophical tradition, but in contrast with most Marxist thinkers, More directly addresses the moral standing of animals. At their religious ceremonies, the Utopians do not sacrifice animals, "for they can't imagine a merciful God enjoying slaughter and bloodshed. They say God gave His creatures life, because He wanted them to live."[79] Any killing of animals is done by the slaves. (That human slavery could one day be abolished was outside even the imagination of an otherwise forward-thinking More). The Utopians themselves are not allowed to do such work since they feel that "slaughtering our fellow-creatures gradually destroys the sense of compassion, which is the finest sentiment of which our human nature is capable."[80]

Hunting animals is considered by the Utopians to be beneath the dignity of free men. More's contempt for sport hunting comes through in this passage from the book: "What pleasure can there be in listening to the barking and yelping of dogs — isn't that rather a disgusting noise? Is there any more real pleasure when a dog chases a rabbit than there is when a dog chases a dog? If what you like is fast running, there's plenty of that in both cases; they're just about the same. But if what you really want is slaughter, if you want to see a living creature torn apart under your eyes, then the whole thing is wrong. You ought to feel nothing but pity when you see the hare fleeing from the hound, the weak creature tormented by the stronger, the fearful and timid beast brutalized by the savage one, the harmless hare killed by the cruel dog."[81]

In More's time, hunting was the national passion of England. Members of all social classes hunted: farmers, laborers, clergy and of course the royal court. It is reported that the young Henry VIII could wear out eight horses during one day's hunting – and, writes one British author, "who was to accuse him of cruelty?"[82] In this context, More's critique of hunting is nothing short of extraordinary. It speaks to his exemplary independence of thought and daring to confront many inhumane customs of his time.

The hunting-critical tradition of Godric and More is alive today. The Hunt Saboteurs Association began in 1963 in the UK, but the movement has since spread to other countries. One early October morning in 1999, a group of Swedish activists walked peacefully in the forest where the annual royal moose hunt was to take place. They were trying to prevent any moose from being shot. The initiative was not appreciated by the hunters.

Carl XVI Gustaf, the king of Sweden, angrily denounced the moose protectors as "mini-Tarzans with Allan Syndrome." The king's frustration was obvious, but the expression confounded commentators. What on earth is Allan Syndrome? people wondered. Whatever the phenomenon is, we may assume that Godric and More suffered from it as well.

God's Children

One group of animals that are victims of prejudice, contempt and persecution are the homeless dogs of the world. Starving, dirty and ragged, they scavenge for food in the garbage. We have met them in cities in Guatemala and Paraguay. They are often shot or poisoned by people who consider them pests.

Shortly after the Peruvian Martin de Porres (1569-1639) had died, testimonies were gathered as part of the process to have him declared a saint. People who had met him spoke of his tenderness toward homeless animals. One monk described how Martin would take wounded animals, mostly dogs, to his cell "and healed them with the same care as if they were rational and he would give them to eat and take care of them until they were well at which point he would ask them to leave."[83] When his superiors forbade him from bringing animals into the monastery, he pleaded for help from his sister Juana, who agreed to open her doors to Martin's animals. He visited her house every day to care for the creatures.

Martin's concern extended also to rodents. After mice ate a hole in the altar cloth at the monastery, one of the monks wanted to set out poison. But Martin defended them: "They are only hungry and are probably trying to build soft nests for their young. Let me see what I can do."[84] He managed to get the mice to move to a shed in the garden, and brought them food daily. Mice and feral dogs – animals at the bottom of society – were objects of Martin's concern. Every creature, according to Martin, was God's *criatura*. The Spanish word means creature, but can also be used to refer to little children. It's probably no coincidence that he used this word. In his theological vision, animals are included among God's children.

Martin also refers to the adult human as God's *criatura*. The theologian Alex García-Rivera claims that the stories of Martin's concern for "irrational" outcasts presented a challenge to the entire social structure of his day – one in which both ecclesiastical and political authorities justified racism and slavery by the specious argument that indigenous Americans possessed less capacity for reason than Spanish and Portuguese colonizers.[85] But more deeply, we believe, Martin's love and care for "irrational" street dogs proclaims this: our neighbors aren't only the ones who look and think like we do. Color of skin, intellectual capacity, and species – such things are not important. In every encounter with an individual in need, God is inviting us to commitment.

Peacemakers

In the early twentieth century a hermit lived on the Greek island of Patmos. At the entrance to his cave, he left bowls of milk for vipers to drink from. One day, some children came from the neighboring village to visit him. When they saw the vipers, they took up stones to kill them with. "Let them be," said the hermit, "they are also God's creatures."[86]

After St Columba had made the sign of the cross over a knife, it could not be used to harm any being. A monk tried to slaughter a bull with one of the blessed knives, but though he pressed hard with the edge of the blade, he was not able to break the animal's skin.[87]

The saints embody God's peace. In their presence, routine acts of violence against animals end. They succeed in establishing peace, even when the odds are against them. According to legend, Martin de Porres managed to get a dog, a cat and a mouse to eat from the same bowl.

In his sermon on the mount, Jesus praises the peacemakers. His followers are encouraged to be creative in building a more just world. Likewise, the fantastic legends of the saints challenge us to boldly and creatively go about building a world without violence, even when people say it is unrealistic. One example of this ingenuity is the trend to replace experiments on animals with alternative methods: tissue cultures instead of live animals to test anti-cancer drugs; computer models taking the place of real frogs in high school biology classrooms; and more.[88] This shows that we can combine scientific advancement with respect for animals.

Aristotle's Influence

Not everyone who has been canonized has stood on the side of animals. The thirteenth century theologian Thomas Aquinas tried to merge traditional Christian faith with the philosophy of Aristotle (who lived three hundred years before Jesus). Aquinas adopted Aristotle's view of animals as resources at the disposal of human beings. "Now, in every government provision is made for the free for their own sake; but for slaves that they may be useful to the free," Aquinas wrote. "Accordingly, the divine providence makes provision for the intellectual creature for its own sake, but for other creatures for the sake of the intellectual creature." All animals were created for the sake of humankind – they have no value in themselves. If any Bible passages "seem to forbid us to be cruel to brute animals," he wrote, "this is either to remove man's thoughts from being cruel to other men, lest through being cruel to animals one become cruel to human beings; or because injury to an animal leads to the temporal hurt of man."[89]

Long before Aquinas, another pre-eminent figure in the western church, Augustine of Hippo (354–430), declared that animals' lack of reason creates an unbridgeable chasm between them and humans. "There are no common rights between us and the beasts," he writes.[90] God's ordained order is for rational creatures – that is, humans – to kill and eat the irrational. Both Aquinas and Augustine were influenced by a Greek philosophical tradition that devalued animals because of their inferior intelligence.[91] This view of animals has dominated the doctrine of the western churches, but the medieval saints don't seem to have cared much about these ancient philosophical ideas. They lived according to the confession that all creatures are important to God.

The medieval era was in many ways a brutal time. Convicted criminals were boiled alive in oil. Traitors were disemboweled, their internal organs thrown onto the fire in front of their eyes. Pigs were also burned alive as punishment for their misdeeds. Brutality towards animals is not surprising for a time when it was commonly acceptable to torture humans.[92] Taking into account the violent times in which they lived, the saints' actions are even more admirable.

Opportunities to Love

When Saint Gertrude the Great (1256—1302) witnessed an animal suffering from hunger, thirst or cold, she would pray to God to have mercy on them and ease their pain.[93] We wonder if anyone ever asked Gertrude how she could care about hungry animals while people were starving.[94] Perhaps she would have answered that one act of compassion does not preclude another. Truly, no human is better off simply because an animal is abused. Nor are love and mercy in such limited supply in the universe that we must decide who is worthy of it and who is not. Isn't it possible to advocate for the hungry people of the world and at the same time care for suffering animals? Or to work for human rights and also practice a compassionate diet?

Why care about animals? Because it is one way to reflect God's love for creation. Why would we say no to an opportunity to express love?

— 7 —
THE LAST SHALL BE THE FIRST: THE REIGN OF GOD

THROUGH HIS WORDS AND ACTIONS, Jesus preached the reign of God. This reign is not what we might expect. Prostitutes enter ahead of the high priests, the last become the first.[95] Where did Jesus learn these values? Luke's gospel might hint at an answer. When Jesus' mother Mary learns that she is pregnant, she offers a prayer of thanks to the God who overturns the social order, the God who has "brought down the powerful from their thrones, and lifted up the lowly."[96]

This perspective comes across in a conversation between Father Zosima and a young man in Dostoyevsky's *The Brothers Karamazov.* "Look at the horse," Zosima said, "that great animal that stands so close to man, or the ox, that nourishes him and works for him, so downcast and pensive, look at their faces: what meekness, what affection for man, who often beats them mercilessly, what mildness, what trustfulness, and what beauty are in that face. It is even touching to know that there is no sin upon them, for everything is perfect, everything except man is sinless, and Christ is with them even before us."

"But can it be that they, too, have Christ?" the young man asked.

"How could it be otherwise," answered Zosima, 'for the Word is for all, all creation and all creatures, every little leaf is striving towards the Word, sings glory to God, weeps to Christ, unbeknownst to itself, doing so through the mystery of its sinless life."[97]

The young man represents humankind in all of its limitations. It's difficult for him to comprehend what Zosima is saying. "But do they too have Christ?" The mere thought that Christ, the Divine Word, would be present in an ox is an unsettling idea. Did he catch the monk saying that Christ is with them *before* us?

Lost Disciples

Jesus' revelation that the last are the first in God's reign is a challenge to those who benefit from the current social order. Even Jesus' closest friends had a difficult time understanding his values. The gospels do not portray the disciples favorably. They look like prisoners of society. They fight among themselves over who is greatest, and they try to use Jesus to advance their own ambitions.[98] They don't understand that discipleship is the way of *service*. Mark's gospel depicts Peter – who would go on to lead the church – as someone who would rather follow Jesus in theory than in practice.[99]

In a popular story from the early Christian community in Egypt, Jesus and his disciples come across a donkey that has been beaten bloody by its owner. The disciples seem unfazed by the animal's suffering. When the owner explains that he bought the animal rightfully and is free to treat it however he wants, the disciples are sympathetic. This upsets Jesus, who turns to them and asks: "Do you then not see how it bleeds, and do you not hear how it groans and cries out?" They answer: "No, Lord, that it groans and cries out, we do not hear."[100]

Because we're born into societies that don't value animals, we usually don't make an effort to find out how they're being treated. We trust the agricultural industry when it says that it cares well for its animals. There are veterinarians on hand, after all, and animal welfare laws.

The donkey Jesus encountered was probably accustomed to suffering in silence. The disciples certainly didn't hear his cries. But the hero of the story did. The challenge for a follower of Christ is to live according to the values of the reign of God – not the status quo. To do so we must listen to voices that aren't easy to hear. We must spend time and interest discovering how animals really live and suffer in laboratories and factory farms. In the inverse order of God's reign, the maltreated ox or mule that no-one seems to hear is a creature of great importance.

The Freedom of the Wild Donkey

The narrator of Milan Kundera's novel *The Unbearable Lightness of Being* reminds us that the Bible was written by a human being, not a horse. God didn't necessarily place humans at the center of creation, with the right to do whatever they want with other animals. "What seems more likely, in fact, is that man invented God to sanctify the dominion that he had usurped for himself over the cow and the horse."[101]

The Bible was written by humans. Every single one of its books views the world from a human point of view. It couldn't be any other way. Only humans have mastered the written word. In the Bible, humankind is treated as the subject and animals as objects. Animals are assistants, servants, pack animals, food, and sacrificial tokens. But sometimes this order is turned on its head. In this passage, God tells Job about someone who has been liberated from torment and given a new life.

> *"Who let the wild donkey go free?*
> *Who untied his ropes?*
> *I gave him the wasteland as his home,*
> *the salt flats as his habitat.*
> *He laughs at the commotion in the town;*
> *he does not hear a driver's shout.*
> *He ranges the hills for his pasture*
> *and searches for any green thing."*[102]

The donkey is no longer an object. *He* is observing the inhabitants of the city, their bustling activity and their driving of his fellow donkeys. And thanks to the care that God has for all creatures, the donkey will not go hungry in this inhospitable desert. The donkey has been "untied," an expression found in Deuteronomy to refer to the freeing of slaves. The donkey is with God, but he has been liberated from the tyranny of his masters.[103]

Francis of Assisi said that "Sister Lark" is "a humble bird, because she gladly goes along the road looking for some grain."[104] Her feathers have the same colors as the earth and her modesty is an example for the disciples of Christ.

In one sense, all animals are humble. They don't try to be something different than they are. They don't know arrogance, pride or haughtiness. "Thank you, God, for the humble," writes a retired Lutheran bishop. "Exalt them to glory."[105] We believe that animals are embraced by that prayer.

– 8 –

THE LEAST OF THESE:
CHRIST'S BIG FAMILY

ANNIKA REMEMBERS: *Her Majesty's Prison Risley, April 1 1999.*

The afternoon sun lit up half of the cell. It was a warm spring day. I opened the window as far as possible, but it didn't make much of a difference. Not even a draft of fresh air reached the bed. The birds were chirping. I relished the spring, as painful as it was to be locked indoors.

Half a year had passed since our disarmament action at the submarine wharf. I was more conscious of the outside world now than during the winter. The weather, the warmth, the birds. I thought about what I could do if I were free: go for a walk or a bicycle tour, pack a lunch and picnic with some friends.

We were on lock-down that day, from 11:30 am onwards due to lack of personnel. The cellblock was quiet. Every now and then a guard walked the corridor, keys rattling with every step.

Sometimes I enjoyed lock-down. I had my own space. I could start something – reading, writing – and know that no one would interrupt me. And of course I knew it wouldn't last forever. Other creatures – the ones locked in cages and crates – aren't so lucky.

In Matthew's gospel, Jesus talks about a great judgment at the end of time. People will face the truth about their lives. Jesus will be the judge, and his measure will be compassion. Jesus will say to those who are good: "I was hungry and you gave me food, I was thirsty and you gave me something to drink, I was a stranger and you welcomed me, I was naked and you gave me clothing, I was sick and you took care of me, I was in prison and you visited me." They will ask in surprise: "Lord, when was it that we saw you hungry and gave you food, or thirsty and gave you something to drink?

And when was it that we saw you a stranger and welcomed you, or naked and gave you clothing? And when was it that we saw you sick or in prison and visited you?"

"Truly I tell you," Jesus will explain, "just as you did it to one of the least of these who are members of my family you did it to me." [106]

Some Bible scholars think that Jesus means by this teaching that he will judge non-Christians for their treatment of Christians. The most common interpretation, however, is that Jesus will judge the whole of humanity – Christians and non-Christians alike – by how they treat any person suffering at the margins of society. [107] It isn't edifying to think that Jesus would only identify with suffering *Christians*. That would conflict with his many examples of border-crossing love. Jesus' God is the parent of all people.

A growing number of Christians are coming to see that God is indeed the parent of all living beings. In this meditation, Carol J. Adams places all suffering beings among "the least of these":

> *"Lord, have we ever seen you suffer as a veal calf? Or imprisoned as a laying hen? Or slaughtered as a fish, or a cow, or a pig?"*

> *"Truly, I tell you, just as you did it to one of the least of these who are members of my family, you did it to me."* [108]

Jesus' family is larger than we have imagined.

The Cosmic Christ

Carol J. Adams is part of a contemporary movement of theologians that is trying to elevate the moral standing of animals. But their ideas are not new. Christian mystics have long seen the suffering of Jesus bound up with the suffering of all creatures. After having a vision of the crucified Christ, Julian of Norwich (1342—1416) reflects on "that instinctive love that creation has to him – and which develops by grace... I saw a close affinity between Christ and ourselves – at least, so I thought – for when he suffered, we suffered. All creatures capable of suffering pain suffered with him."[109] Whenever the English mystic Margery Kempe (1373 — 1440) witnessed a horse being whipped, she saw Christ being whipped again.[110]

This mystical insight also surfaces in a poem by Edith Sitwell (1887–1964). "He bears in his heart all wounds," she writes about the suffering Christ – who continues to suffer in the world through the "wounds of the baited bear – / The blind and weeping bear whom the keepers beat / On his helpless flesh ... the tears of the hunted hare."[111]

Julian, Kempe, and Sitwell witness to the cosmic Christ, the One who gathers into himself the whole of the universe. In the New Testament, Christ is described as the "Divine Word" through which "all things came into being." Through his death on the cross, "God was pleased to reconcile to Himself all things, whether on earth or in heaven."[112] These New Testament passages serve as a foundation for understanding Christ's all-encompassing work of redemption. Not only does Christ suffer with animals; his death also serves them. "Christ shed his blood for kine and horses ... as well as for men," claimed the English religious dissident William Bowling in 1646.[113] The diarist Ralph Josselin wrote in 1655 that Christ was born in a stable because he was "the redeemer of man and beast out of their bondage by the Fall."[114]

God is present in all creation, yet hidden. Creation is God's disguise.[115] We see this notion of God's secretive presence in Matthew's judgment scene. The triune God meets us in the oppressed, the needy, "the least of these." In humans, yes; and also in the afflicted animals of the world.

9

CARING FOR THE LITTLE ONES:
ON CHILDREN AND ANIMALS

THAT CHILDREN HAVE RIGHTS is a relatively new idea. In ancient Palestine, children were powerless under their parents' control – without any legal protections. They were considered adults-in-the-making, and had no real value as people until the age of 12 or 13. It was common place for parents to beat their children, and Scripture seemed to encourage it. "Do not withhold discipline from a child," says one of the Proverbs, "if you punish him with the rod, he will not die. Punish him with the rod and save his soul from death."[116] Children suffered in other parts of the Roman Empire, as well. According to the historian Dionysios of Halikarnassos (b. ca. 60 BCE), "the law-giver of the Romans gave virtually full power to the father over his son, whether he thought proper to imprison him, to scourge him, to put him in chains, and keep him at work in the fields, or to put him to death."[117]

But Jesus defended children. When a group of families with young children tried to approach Jesus, his disciples scolded them and turned them away. Jesus "was indignant" at the sight of this, and told his disciples: "Let the little children come to me; do not stop them; for it is to such as these that the kingdom of God belongs."[118] This passage must be understood against the background of children's low social status. New Testament scholar Judith Gundry-Volf writes that "children's vulnerability and powerlessness seem to lie at the heart of Jesus' extension of the reign of God to them."[119]

"Who is the greatest in the kingdom of heaven?" the disciples once wanted to know. So Jesus called a little child to sit with them. "I tell you the truth," he answered, "unless you change and become like little children, you will never enter the kingdom of heaven."[120] This change – this conversion – requires that we side with those who are powerless and see reality with their eyes, writes the Lutheran theologian Per Frostin.[121]

Each generation of Christians must map out their own time and culture, in order to identify who is powerless and to try to see the world from their perspective.

Whipped Like a Dog

Children and animals have both suffered at the bottom of the social hierarchy. Sometimes they have been the victims of similar violence. Obey me and your mother, a grandfather ordered a four-year-old boy in 1739, "or I will whip you like a dog which is being trained."[122]

Children have even been viewed as animals themselves. "What is an infant," asked a seventeenth century English author, "but a brute beast in the shape of a man?" Children's language was "no little, if at all, better than the sounds the most sagacious brute animals make to each other."[123] In 1638, the famous theologian Thomas Hooker remarked that children don't have the capacity to understand "the mysteries of life and salvation," and therefore lived the "life of a beast."[124]

We can learn several lessons from this aspect of our history.

First of all, power corrupts. Adults have enjoyed unlimited power over children and animals, but haven't lived up to the responsibility that comes with it. The moral sensitivities of many adults have been corrupted – an easy trap when the weaker party can't even speak in its own defense.

Secondly, the capacity to reason has been overemphasized as a standard for judging the moral worth of an individual. Throughout western history, many philosophers have claimed that adult humans have a unique dignity because of our intellect. This is done at the expense of animals who, according to the German philosopher Immanuel Kant (1724–1804), "are there merely as a means to an end. That end is man."[125]

This isn't only a problem of secular philosophers. Many Christians have also promoted human uniqueness on the basis of our free will and ability to act according to reason.[126] The classic 1913 *Catholic Encyclopedia* explains that only "a being possessed of reason and self-control, can be the subject of rights and duties." The author of this entry warns against "unduly magnifying, to the neglect of higher duties, our obligations concerning animals."[127]

We should be grateful for the capacity to reason. It can help us solve many difficult problems. But intellect shouldn't be the measure of an individual's value. There are those who do not have intellectual faculties to the same extent as an average adult human. These are not less valuable.

Animals and Children as Prophets

The intellect has been exalted within and outside of the church. But you can also see the contours of an alternative perspective, where nonrational beings are upheld as exemplary. In his account of Jesus' life, Matthew writes: "The blind and the lame came to him in the temple, and he cured them. But when the chief priests and the scribes saw the amazing thing that he did, and heard the children crying out in the temple, 'Hosanna to the Son of David,' they became angry and said to him, 'Do you hear what these are saying?' Jesus said to them, 'Yes; have you never read, Out of the mouths of infants and nursing babies you have prepared praise for yourself'?"[128] The children in the temple, Gundry-Volf points out, "play the striking role of those who have true insight about Jesus." They understand what the priests do not: Jesus is the Messiah.[129] Earlier in Matthew's gospel, Jesus says that God has hidden the signs of the messianic reign "from the wise and the intelligent," but "revealed them to infants."[130]

A striking parallel to the story of the children in the temple is found in the *Gospel of Pseudo-Matthew*, an influential medieval work based on earlier accounts of Jesus' youth. It tells the story of an eight-year old Jesus coming across a pack of lions who "ran to meet Him, and adored Him." The people who witnessed this "stood at a distance, on account of the lions; for they did not dare to come close to them." Then Jesus said to the people: "How much better are the beasts than you, seeing that they recognize their Lord, and glorify Him; while you men, who have been made after the image and likeness of God, do not know Him! Beasts know me, and are tame; men see me, and do not acknowledge me."[131]

Concern for Animals and Children

"The reasons for legal intervention in favour of children apply not less strongly to the case of those unfortunate slaves and victims of the most brutal part of mankind – the lower animals," wrote the English philosopher John Stuart Mill in 1848.[132] These sentiments were shared by many people in England and the United States in the nineteenth century. In 1884, Henry Bergh, a leader in the animal welfare movement in New York (known by many as "the Great Meddler"), was asked to help a tormented "little animal" – which turned out to be a little girl. The girl had been brutally abused by her foster parents. Bergh intervened and successfully persuaded the courts to release her from their custody. Moved by the experience, Bergh later founded the New York Society for the Prevention of Cruelty to Children. When news of this reached activists with the Royal Society for the Prevention of Cruelty of Animals in London, they established a similar organization.[133]

"The protection of children and the protection of animals," argued the Colorado Bureau of Child and Animal Protection, "are combined because of the principle involved, i.e. their helplessness, is the same; because all life is the same, differing only in degree of development and expression; and because each profits by association with the other." By 1909, 185 humane organizations in the United States were working for the protection of both animals and children.[134]

We can uncover traces of this tradition even today. A web site dedicated to Saint Jude, for instance, allows people to post prayers for "the innocents in this world who are not in a position to help themselves," including "abandoned children" and "mistreated animals."[135]

The theological motivation for this dynamic can be found in Andrew Linzey's understanding of the moral priority of the weak. Children can't defend themselves and their needs in the same way as adults. Neither can animals. Therefore, adults must give special consideration to the needs of both.[136]

Without Guilt, Yet Victims

"I need to beg forgiveness, to make myself pure and fit for God," reads an eighth century poem. "But the blackbird who drinks with me from the stream sheds no tears of contrition; he is as God made him, with no stain of sin."[137]

Animals and young children share a lack of moral guilt. "Man, do not exalt yourself above the animals," proclaims the monk Zosima, "they are sinless, and you, you with your grandeur, fester the earth by your appearance on it, and leave your festering trace behind you – alas, almost every one of us does!"[138]

Animals are not responsible for the problems and miseries of the world. Humans suffer diseases and natural disasters – animals are without guilt in it. Humans despoil the earth and make war – animals are without guilt in it.

Much of animal research today is meant to find cure for problems that have been caused by our own poor choices. Animals don't smoke, yet scientists at the University of California forced mice to inhale tobacco smoke for five months to assess the link between smoking and lung tumors in humans.[139] Animals don't wage war, yet military scientists around the world test the effects of chemical weapons on rats, primates, pigs, rabbits, and other animals.[140]

"But tell us, O Man!" say the birds in a 1683 treatise by Thomas Tryon, "we pray you tell us what injuries have we committed to forfeit? What law have we broken, or what Cause given you, whereby you can pretend a Right to invade and violate our part, and natural Rights, and to assault and destroy us, as if we were the Agressors and no better than Thieves, Robbers and Murtherers, fit to be extirpated out of the Creation?"[141] The birds are correct in their complaint. They haven't broken any law. Neither they nor the mice used at the University of California have injured us, yet we "assault and destroy" them.

To make others pay (with their lives), for the miseries we brought upon ourselves is unfair – even evil. Cardinal John Henry Newman (1801–90) wrote that "there is something so very dreadful, so Satanic in tormenting those who have never harmed us, and who cannot defend themselves, who are utterly in our power."[142]

The modern animal rights movement was born in the middle of the 1970s. It has primarily focused on abolishing industrial animal agriculture, painful animal experiments and fur farming. Some critics have called these demands "extreme." But are they? We teach our children that they shouldn't use violence, especially against those who are weaker than they. This is a basic and commonly held moral principle, reflected in expressions like "don't kick a man when he's down." Our disgust for the abuse of the weak by the strong is deep-set. It's manifest in the instinct to spontaneously intervene when a child or animal is hurt. Unfortunately, we aren't consistent. We react strongly when little boys tear the wings off of flies, but not when adults lock animals into small cages and conduct painful experiments on them.

The ethical demands of the animal rights movement are not extreme. They can be characterized as a consistent application of the moral framework we have all long embraced.

10

ALL BEINGS CRY OUT TO YOU:
THE DEATH AND RESURRECTION OF "BOJAN"

PELLE REMEMBERS: *I was running. It was after midnight and the spruce trees towered ominously on either side of the gravel road. It felt wrong to be running. It's one of the standard rules for non-violent action: no running, no shouting, no sudden movements. But what was I to do? Valuable time had been lost, so I urged myself along. After all, no-one saw me. The neighborhood lay still, people were sleeping. All I heard was my panting and footsteps hitting the gravel.*

Meanwhile, the others waited in the minivan. It was my task to lead us to the right place. We were off schedule and couldn't find the farm. How unprofessional can we get? And I was the person responsible for organizing and training the group! I tried to smile at the embarrassing situation.

I was sweating through my coveralls. My boots felt clumsy.

The others were sitting silently when I returned. "Okay, the training continues," I said. "Pay attention to this! If you are doing recon in the daytime, remember that the place looks entirely different at night."

We took another route and soon a farm yard opened in front of us, with a low, windowless, red building.

"This isn't the place," I said.

"Are you sure?"

"Yes. It could be an egg farm, but this isn't where we were."

Should we do the rescue here, anyhow? We turned the engine off. The building was lit, but there didn't seem to be any houses nearby. What did people think? Personally, I was at a loss for what to do next.

"I think we should do it," Petter said.

There were no hens there. After we had pried open the door, I peaked inside: turkeys were standing tightly together in an area about the size of a basketball court. Well, you could have suspected that this is how it is for turkeys, I remember thinking. On a piece of paper, I wrote an explanation to the owners. I told them who we were and how they could contact us.

All nine of us climbed back into the van and drove off.

People had come from all over the country to take part in this rescue. We had a training during the day. In the role plays we had practiced what we would do if caught by the owner, how we were to greet him respectfully. We also talked about democracy, about why it is important to obey laws, but also when it may be necessary to break a law. In a round everyone had a chance to talk about her or his fears about the consequences of our civil disobedience. We prepared the cardboard boxes and had written a letter to those who work at the farm. From the payphone at the square I phoned the three sanctuaries one last time. They could take care of thirty-six hens. What if we didn't find the place after all of that!

How we found it I don't remember, but it was a quarter of a mile away. The outer door was unlocked. The first thing I saw was a pile of dead hens. They lay to our left as we entered. I registered them for a fraction of a second before the first row of cages rising up toward the ceiling captured my attention: they were empty.

They had to be further inside. With the boxes in our hands, we moved quickly along a narrow passageway next to the wall. The air offered resistance. The stench of ammonia invaded our nostrils. It was like pushing yourself through a viscous wall. I had never experienced anything like it.

The hens sat in the next corridor. Twelve thousand, the papers wrote afterwards.

On the way out, I didn't think of the pile of dead hens. We were in a hurry and were concertedly carrying the boxes, each with three to four hens. Not until I saw a photograph from the action did they return to my consciousness. Brown and white bodies by turn. Their heads were cut off, their faces gone. Only bodies with stiffly spread wings.

A year later we faced trial, charged with theft. My fellow activists were sentenced to two years suspended sentence and a fine. Since I had previously received a suspended sentence, I was sentenced to a month in prison. Upon leaving the court house, I was proud of what we'd done. I did not feel *at all discouraged. In comparison to the terrible treatment of battery hens, a month spent behind bars didn't seem so unbearable. I was determined to continue these kinds of rescue actions.*

The Bible testifies that animals turn to their creator with their needs, trusting and praising God.[143] This theme was picked up by Gregory of Nazianzus (ca 330–389). "All creation sings the glory of God in wordless strain," he wrote, adding that "the whole of the animal kingdom is smiling."[144] Gregory also composed this song of praise:

> *All things cry about you*
> *those which speak, and those which cannot speak,*
> *all things honor you,*
> *those which think, and those which cannot think.*
> *For there is one longing, one groaning, that all things have*
> *for you.*
>
> *All things pray to you that comprehend your plan*
> *and offer you a silent hymn.*[145]

The idea that all creatures live in devotion to God was shared by other early Christians. "The whole creation prays," writes Tertullian (160–225). "Cattle and wild beasts pray, and bend their knees, and in coming forth from their stalls and lairs look up to heaven, their mouth not idle, making the spirit move in their own fashion. Moreover the birds taking flight lift themselves up to heaven and instead of hands spread out the cross of their wings, while saying something which may be supposed to be a prayer."[146]

If Tertullian and Gregory are correct, then what muted words are cried out from the throats of the imprisoned? Many dairy cows stand chained by their necks to a concrete floor, incapable of normal movement.[147] Stand up. Lay down. Dreariness. Monotony. What is contained in the call of the cow? Or the battery hen, when her plumage has been rubbed off against the steal cage? Do songs of praise still rise from her beak?

Psalms of Retribution

The Psalms are a collection of prayers to God. Among them are Psalms of retribution that beg God to curse and punish the enemy. "O LORD, the God who avenges, O God who avenges shine forth."[148] To those who "mete out violence on the earth," the psalmist asks: "Break the teeth in their mouths, O God."[149]

After rescuing 36 battery caged hens – the story mentioned in the beginning of this chapter – Pelle and the other activists left a home-baked cake for the farm employees. On another rescue, the owner got a box of chocolates. All work for a better world should have a human face. The rebel should be friendly. Confrontation with oppression should be combined with care, even for those who are involved directly in an immoral business. The opponent should never be demonized.

From this perspective, the bloodthirsty theology of the Psalms is unacceptable. At the same time, the psalmist's harsh words contain a lesson for us today. Caesarius Cavallin, abbot of a Lutheran monastery in Sweden, reminds us that the Psalms were written in a time where the law was often synonymous with the will of the powerful, and where violence had the last word.[150] In a modern, democratic society founded on the rule of law, it is easy to be restrained and civilized. We are not generally tempted to resort to merciless revenge. But the powerless are still among us, suffering oppression with no end to their misery in sight. That is why these Psalms still have a place in our devotional lives. They speak about and give expression to a desperate situation: how the mighty mistreat the weak without being held accountable.

Where are psalms of retribution prayed today? Through what mouths do the curses sound? Our thoughts go to the factory farms that we have visited, to the animals, to "those which speak, and those which cannot speak." The hen that pushes against the steel cage without understanding why she is there, without knowing whether she will ever be free. She can't even escape her prison through her imagination. She has no memory of sand baths, scratching the earth, or caring for her young.[151] Prayers originating from such a situation might require strong words. "The LORD lifts up the downtrodden; he casts the wicked to the ground."[152] There is so much rage and anguish in these Psalms. When we pray them, we share in the suffering, if only for a moment. We pray the Psalms in solidarity with the oppressed, joining our voices to their cry to the Lord of Hosts, that God will one day establish justice.

The Psalms also stand as a warning to Bible readers in all times: are there defenseless individuals suffering violence in your society? If so, what are you going to do about it? Your decision will have consequences as you stand before the Holy One.

Resting in the Blueberry Bush

"When we do not know how to pray properly," Paul writes in his letter to the Romans, "then the Spirit personally makes our petitions for us in groans that cannot be put into words."[153] This supports the reflections of Gregory and Tertullian about the prayer lives of animals. Advanced verbal skills are not as important to God as we humans might think. Even if animals cannot put words to their prayers, the spirit intercedes on their behalf.

Paul declares that "creation itself will be set free from its bondage to decay and will obtain the freedom of the glory of the children of God. We know that the whole creation has been groaning in labor pains until now."[154] He looks forward to a time in which God's will has been fully realized, for all creatures. Of the thirty-six hens that were rescued, five were taken to a sanctuary outside of Stockholm. Chatarina Krångh describes their new life on her land. We read her story as a glimpse into the coming renewal of creation:

"Although it was warm and sunny, they didn't dare go out for the first two days. They sat on the straw- and peat-covered floor of the new hen house. In the morning of the third day, the first hen took a step outside and soon the others followed.

"I stood there experiencing a holy moment. I saw how they, as they were hit by the warming rays of the morning sun, turned their eyes up to that inviting source of warmth and lay down. They stretched their wings

55

and experienced a sun bath for the first time in their lives. Neither I nor my girlfriend could hold back our tears.

"We named one of the hens Bojan. In the beginning she was skittish – the slightest movement or sound frightened her. But her natural curiosity took over. Together with her sisters, she looked for food in the forest, took refreshing sand baths and scratched the earth. She ran and she slumbered among the blueberry bushes.

"The egg industry ruthlessly breeds laying hens to be as productive as possible. This is done at the expense of the hens' health. Their ovaries become overworked. Bojan was no exception. A little better than two years after her rescue, a tumor began growing in her ovary. To better care for her, we let her stay with us. During the daytime she moved freely in the yard, at night she preferred our house. Her nest, a cat carrier, sat on the floor in our kitchen. Every morning Helena and I were greeted with happy clucking as we came for breakfast. Bojan ate when we ate, and she sat nestled against my legs when we were watching TV. She loved to be petted and would stretch out her neck and close her eyes as I caressed her under the beak.

"One Sunday in May, we took a last walk in the garden. I was poking in the dirt and she was close to me, scratching and looking for food. When evening came, she went into her nest and fell asleep.

"The next morning we went to the veterinary hospital where she would undergo an operation. The last month she had become more and more affected by her tumor. She tired easily. From having been very social, she grew withdrawn. The chances that she would get well again were not good, but we wanted to do everything we could to save her.

"Bojan lay still in her carrier as I brought her to the hospital.

"The operation was successful and the tumor was completely removed. But she had barely woken when she closed her eyes again, forever. Her heart was too weak. We picked her up in the evening and drove home in the dusk.

"Early the next morning we buried Bojan in a glade in the forest."[155]

Echoing Paul's letter to the Romans, the English diarist John Evelyn wrote, in 1677: "even the creatures should enjoy a manumission [emancipation] and as much felicity as their nature is capable of, when at the last day they shall no longer groan for their servitude to sinful man."[156] Over three hundred years later, in the age of industrialized animal agriculture, this message is more relevant than ever. We can't rid the world of sin nor achieve heavenly bliss. But we can be a part of the liberation of God's creatures. Such a contribution is deeply meaningful in itself, but at the same time it serves as a way to prepare for the God that meets us from the future. It is a prelude, an opening score, to the completion of creation that awaits.

$-$ 11 $-$
WHAT WOULD
JESUS EAT?

IN JOSÉ SARAMAGO'S NOVEL *The Gospel According to Jesus Christ*, Jesus walks into the Temple to sacrifice a lamb. He is suddenly seized with disgust in the face of all the blood and slaughter. He chooses to let the lamb live, an act that has ripple effects in his daily life: "deep inside he felt uneasy, from now on he would face the awkward contradiction between eating lambs and refusing to kill them."[157]

The Portuguese author, who was awarded the Nobel Prize for literature in 1998, hasn't been the only one to give some thought to what Jesus did or didn't eat. When Annika told a friend of hers that she didn't eat fish, the woman exclaimed: "But Jesus gave fish and bread to the crowds!" During his seminary studies, one of Pelle's classmates reflected: "When I was a teenager and deciding whether or not to be a vegetarian, I asked myself what my idol – Jesus – ate. And he surely ate meat. So I never became a vegetarian."

Other Christians have claimed that Jesus was a vegetarian. At the turn of the twentieth century, the English priest G. J. R. Ouseley (1835–1906), wrote a gospel in which Jesus advocates a diet of fruit and of herbs: "And, for thy living, behold the fields yielding their increase, and the fruit-bearing trees and the herbs: what needest thou more than these which honest work of thy hands will not give thee? Woe to the strong who misuse their strength. Woe to the crafty who hurt the creatures of God. Woe to the hunters, for they shall be hunted."[158] In Ouseley's account, Jesus fed the multitude with five melons.

In the same spirit, the American animal rights organization People for the Ethical Treatment of Animals (PETA) launched a "Jesus was a vegetarian" campaign. Their proposition didn't go unchallenged. In an article about the campaign, the Los Angeles Times interviewed Russell Moore, an assistant professor at the Southern Baptist Theological Seminary in Louisville, Kentucky. "No diet should invoke Jesus," Moore said. "He nowhere universalized his diet any more than he advocates wearing robes and sandals." He called the campaign "an attempt to co-opt Jesus for left-wing animal rights propaganda."[159] Many Christian animal rights advocates also reacted negatively. The Anglican priest Andrew Linzey, a leading Christian animal rights theologian, called the campaign "misguided, even counterproductive."[160]

People clearly have strong opinions about Jesus' diet. In this chapter we will discuss Jesus, his eating habits, and their relevance for today's Christians. To do this, we must first consider the book in which the stories of Jesus are collected: the Bible.

"I do as it says in the Bible." "In this congregation, we are faithful to the Bible." Some Christians think that reading the Bible is uncomplicated: you read it and do what it says. But the Bible is a book, and as one scholar points out, no book "says" anything. "Put your ear next to the book and you'll notice that it is utterly silent!" It is the reader who gives voice to the book, but only once it has "passed through the reader's brain and met the knowledge and experiences that are stored there!"[161] All Bible reading is inevitably a question of translation, selection, and interpretation.

Translation.

An English-language New Testament has been subject to two stages of translation. The first happened when the evangelists put the oral tradition about Jesus, who spoke Aramaic, into written Greek. The second happened when scholars transposed the Greek gospels into modern English. Sometimes well-meaning Christians will ask bible scholars to just translate the gospels as they are written. But it isn't so easy. Translation always involves interpretation. Sometimes a Greek word won't translate directly, or will have multiple possible meanings. In these cases, both tradition and the translators' own worldview and theology will influence their understanding of the passage. Here are a few examples.

Among the people that Jesus praises in his sermon on the mount are the "meek" – at least according to most English translations. But a few translations (New Jerusalem Bible and Scholars Version) translate the same original Greek word as "gentle." "Meek" and "gentle" mean different things in English: on one hand, docility and powerlessness, on the other, active compassion.

Later in the same sermon, Jesus teaches his followers how to respond to violence. In the New International Version, Jesus says: "You have heard that it was said, 'an eye for an eye and a tooth for a tooth.' But I say to you, Do not resist an evildoer."[162] Biblical scholar Walter Wink argues that the passivity of "Do not resist an evildoer" is quite different from Jesus' original message. In this case, the Greek word translated as "resist" suggests a violent rebellion. According to Wink, Jesus was in fact encouraging an occupied people to engage in creative, nonviolent resistance. The passage should more properly be translated as "Do not retaliate against violence with violence."[163] The Scholars Version offers a similar translation: "Don't react violently against the one who is evil."

Translations from Hebrew to English involve the same set of problems. In the second chapter of Genesis, the original Hebrew text uses the term nephesh chayah ("living being" or "living creature") to describe both humans and animals at the point of creation. But two prominent English translations (the New Revised Standard Version and New International Version) make a distinction that does not exist in the original. In both cases, nephesh chayah is rendered as "living being" when referring to humans, but as "living creature" when referring to animals.[164]

Selection.

Everyone reads the Bible selectively. No one attributes the same weight to all verses of the Bible. The Roman Catholic Church has emphasized gospel texts that lend support to the papacy and priestly celibacy. The Lutheran church has lifted up Paul's writings about people being "justified by faith" (Gal 3:24). With this as a filter for interpretation, other New Testament texts have been pushed aside. Luther didn't like the letter of James, for example, which highlights the importance of good works.

Selectivity only becomes a problem if we aren't conscious of it. If we believe that we are uninfluenced by our own prejudices and worldview, we deceive ourselves. No Christian should have to do that.

After the great flood, God established a new covenant with all the inhabitants of the earth. This covenant is often referred to as God's covenant "with all humanity," or "with all peoples."[165] But the ninth chapter of the book of Genesis actually states – five times – that the covenant is between God and "every living creature." We should stop to ask ourselves why we so often close our eyes to those passages in which animals have a role.

Interpretation.

The Trinity is a central doctrine in most Christian churches. It means that God is one, but at the same time three persons: usually expressed as Father, Son and Holy Spirit. This idea gradually developed over the first few centuries of church history, and became fixed doctrine in the fourth century. One might expect that such a fundamental doctrine would find unanimous and clear support in the gospels. But this isn't the case. In fact, Jesus expressly denies that he is morally perfect or of divine nature. When he was addressed as "Good Teacher" he answered: "Why do you call me good? No one is good but God alone."[166]

Krister Stendahl, former Dean of Harvard Divinity School, calls the Trinity "the boldest of interpretations in classical Christianity."[167] It testifies to the fact that earlier generations of Christians were uninhibited in their interpretation of the contents of the Christian faith. It is a continuous reminder of the right and obligation of Christians to, in all times, deeply reflect on what we believe.

The Bible is no monolith. It is a collection of sixty-six books (or seventy-six, seventy-seven, or seventy-eight, depending on the version), written over a period of hundreds of years. Different books present different worldviews and ethical frameworks. There isn't always theological unity among them. Some texts criticize others.[168] The books express many different interpretations of the divine reality.

The gospels present four different views of Jesus. Mark's Jesus is not the same as John's Jesus.[169] And then there are the epistles. Paul's writings almost entirely lack quotes from Jesus, or references to Jesus as an historical person. He creates a picture of Jesus which deviates in many ways from those of the four evangelists. Paul's "gospel" adds to the diversity of interpretations of Jesus in the New Testament. This diversity contributes to the complexity of Biblical interpretation. We can't, in any simple way, determine what "the Bible says" about a particular issue.

And what about the ugly ideas contained within the Bible? John's gospel has many contemptuous references to "the Jews" (although Jesus himself was Jewish). On one occasion, Jesus is quoted as saying to "the Jews": "You are from your father the devil, and you chose to do your father's desires."[170] Bible quotes like this one were used by Christian Nazis to stir up anti-semitic hatred. "No one recognized the nature of Judaism more clearly nor fought it more single-mindedly," wrote one German religious textbook from 1940, "than precisely Jesus the Savior."[171] Facing trial after the war, one prominent Nazi said in his defense: "Only the Jews had remained victorious after the dreadful days of World War I. These were the people of whom Christ said: 'Their father is the devil.'"[172] The anti-Jewish images of Christ stand as a terrible reminder that even the hero of the gospels can be used for bad purposes. A person can't settle a social or moral question simply by quoting Jesus.

Signs of Good Interpretation

As we have shown, the Bible can be used to support a number of different – and often contradictory – points of view. Therefore it's important to have guidelines for acceptable interpretation. Bible scholar and Lutheran theologian Jesper Svartvik suggests that love should be the ultimate criterion for interpretation. "Surely, one guiding principle ought to be that textual interpretation encourage a way of thinking and acting that reflects the divine love."[173]

This way of reading Scripture is rooted in the teachings of Jesus, who said that the most important commandment is to love God and neighbor. He also said that the most important matters of the law were "justice and mercy and faith."[174] Justice and mercy are essential components of self-giving love.

Pedophiles sometimes justify their acts of abuse as acts of love. But love promotes the other's physical and mental health, a condition that child abuse can never live up to. It isn't enough, then, to refer to love. We need more clarification. Self-giving love requires that we see, acknowledge and respond to the needs of others. The good Samaritan did that when he cared for the man on the roadside. That's why Jesus praised him as someone who "loved his neighbor."

Violence is not consistent with self-giving love. There are many Bible passages that support violence, genocide, imperialism, the death penalty, child abuse, oppression of women and homosexuals, and violence against animals. According to the criterion of love, such texts should not be guiding lights for us. We believe that any use of the Bible to encourage violence against humans or animals is reprehensible.

It is wrong, writes Svartvik, for an influential group to use "a small number of texts to oppress, humiliate and persecute another group."[175] He refers to Christians who use the Bible to attack people in gay or lesbian relationships. But this principle can also be applied to the oppression of animals. People cite a few Bible texts to legitimize the imprisonment, force-feeding and killing of members of other species.

The Possessed and the Herd of Swine

One day, Jesus meets a man possessed by "unclean" spirits. The spirits recognize Jesus and beg him not to destroy them, but to send them instead into a large herd of swine that is feeding nearby. "And the unclean spirits came out and entered the swine; and the herd, numbering about 2,000, rushed down the steep bank into the sea, and were drowned in the sea."[176]

This passage has been used for hundreds of years to justify violence against animals. Augustine of Hippo (354–430) cites this story, and another episode in which Jesus cursed a fig tree, to argue that Jesus didn't care about animals and plants. "Christ himself shows that to refrain from the killing of animals and the destroying of plants is the height of superstition, for judging that there are no common rights between us and the beasts and trees, he sent the devils into a herd of swine and with a curse withered the tree on which he found no fruit.... Surely the swine had not sinned, nor had the tree."[177]

At the time the gospels were written, people thought that mental illnesses were caused by demons. Demonic possession would have been a perfectly natural explanation for a large herd of swine rushing to their deaths. But today we must not – indeed, we cannot – think exactly like people did in antiquity. Our perspectives have changed as a result of increased knowledge about ourselves and the world. The Lutheran bishop Ingemar Ström (1912–2002) offers some insight into what could have been the background for this peculiar episode. When the man came rushing and screaming toward Jesus, even the swine were terrified and fled in panic. "Whoever has heard how pigs can scream at those occasions can imagine the scene. Aha, people thought, now the devil has entered the swine, and thus a story emerges."[178]

Others question whether this event ever happened. Different gospels give slightly different versions of the story, and place it in different locations. According to one theory, this is a political story that grew out of anti-Roman sentiment. The demon says to Jesus that its name is Legion – the name for the largest Roman military unit. The spirits beg Jesus not to "send them out of the country." The swine (unclean animals) can be interpreted as symbols for the "unclean" conquerors that had occupied Jewish lands. The self-destruction of the possessed swine then is a symbol for the end of occupation, when the Roman soldiers have been sent "out of the country."[179]

There are Christians who think that the event took place the way it is described. For some, the story is an example of how a serious follower of Jesus cannot ascribe any high value to animals. "If our Lord felt it OK to sacrifice 2000 higher mammals to save the life of one man," writes one Christian defender of animal experimentation, "I believe he would condone, no, DEMAND experiments which may save the lives of thousands of people!"[180]

PELLE REMEMBERS: *One year in the early 1990s, I spent a Christmas break with my parents at their home in Kent, in southeastern England. As my mother prepared dinner in the kitchen, I sat upstairs reading a book about liberation theology that I had purchased in London. The author, a prominent Christian thinker, reflected on the text on the possessed man and the herd of swine. Through his action, Jesus shows that he values human life more than personal property, he explained. Two thousand swine, that was a large fortune. "What a good interpretation," I thought. "Striking! I'll be sure to remember that." It didn't cross my mind that the swine could be seen as anything other than a rich person's possessions.*

The Passover Lamb

Scholars have long recognized that the four gospels are not reliable sources of information on the historical Jesus, the person who once walked in Galilee and Judea. The evangelists were not critical historians or biographers. Writing several decades after Jesus' death, they saw him through "the filter of the resurrection." They wanted to convince others that Jesus was, indeed, the son of God who had risen from the dead.

We're limited in our knowledge of what the historical Jesus said and did. The answer to the question of what kinds of food Jesus ate is more or less a matter of well-founded assumption. Historically certain conclusions aren't to be found.

Only one story in the gospels describes Jesus eating animals. At the end of Luke's gospel, the resurrected Jesus appears to some disciples and answers their disbelief by saying to them: "Look at my hands and my feet; see that it is I, myself. Touch me and see; for a ghost does not have flesh and bones as you see that I have." He asks for something to eat and they hand him a piece of broiled fish. Jesus "took it and ate it in their presence."[181] In the last chapter of John's gospel, Jesus appears in a similar fashion to the disciples, but in this story it is he who offers them bread and fish to eat.

Many scholars think that these stories grew out of theological disputes within the early church. Some groups were saying that the earthly body of Jesus was just a mirage: he was of pure divine nature. Others argued that Jesus was fully human and fully divine, and that he had resurrected bodily. This latter group used stories of Jesus eating food after his resurrection as evidence of their position. After all, pure spirit can't chew and swallow food.[182]

But is it likely that Jesus would have been portrayed eating fish if he had in real life been a strict vegetarian? American theologian and vegetarian advocate Stephen Webb doesn't think so, and concludes that Jesus probably ate fish.[183]

Christian Vegetarian Association chair Stephen Kaufman, M.D. notes that Luke's Gospel was written decades after Jesus died, and the Gentile community to which Luke addressed his Gospel had little direct knowledge about Jesus. It is possible that they knew little about Jesus' actual diet and would not have found a story about Jesus eating fish unbelievable, even if he had been a vegetarian.

Lamb is an integral part of the Jewish feast of Passover, commemorating Israel's liberation from slavery in Egypt. According to Mark, Matthew and Luke, Jesus' last meal was a Passover celebration. But they only mention bread and wine as part of the meal. Why didn't they mention the lamb? Perhaps there wasn't any need – everyone had lamb at Passover, so it would just be stating the obvious. But it could also be that there was no lamb, since Jesus himself filled that role. He would be slaughtered – crucified – to fulfill God's new act of liberation. This symbolism would be weakened if there were another lamb at the table.[184]

The Freedom of a Christian

Most modern animal rights theologians assume that Jesus ate much like everyone else in his time – meaning he ate meat. But that doesn't settle the issue of how we should eat today. In his book *Animal Theology*, Andrew Linzey reminds us that Christian discipleship cannot consist of mechanically imitating the historical Jesus – a Jew who lived in first century Palestine. We have great freedom to apply our Christian faith in many different ways, so long as it's consistent with the self-giving example of Jesus.

Linzey also says that we should take a lesson from the doctrine of the Incarnation – a Latin word that literally means "in the flesh." All glory, knowledge and power are God's, yet God chose to "became flesh" in Jesus of Nazareth. No single human life, not even Jesus, can manifest all aspects of self-giving love. Those who complain that Jesus didn't advocate vegetarianism, or more forcefully confront patriarchy, slavery and Roman occupation forget that "to confess Christ crucified is to confess a Christ inevitably and profoundly limited by the fact of incarnation. To be in one place at one time means that one cannot be everywhere."[185]

It's uncertain whether any ethical vegetarian movements existed in Palestine at the time of Jesus. Vegetarianism was then generally associated with Gnosticism, a religious movement that had a negative view of creation, the body, and bodily functions. Gnostics thought that whoever ate animal flesh was defiled because animals are created through the evil of sexual intercourse. They abstained from meat, alcohol and sex as a way of starving demons out of their bodies.

The irony, points out New Testament scholar Richard Alan Young, is that the Gnostics' negative view of animals led them to avoid eating meat, while our society's negative view of animals leads to unrestrained consumption of flesh. Leaders of the early church condemned the Gnostics and their ascetic rejection of animal foods. In the same spirit, Young suggests that Christians today should condemn animal cruelty, since it also diminishes the goodness of God's creation.[186]

Jesus didn't eat pork, Stephen Webb points out, but most of his followers today don't seem to care about that. Nor do Christians limit themselves to traditional Middle Eastern food, although that's what Jesus ate. We don't express our faith by copying Jesus' daily habits. Instead, we listen to his teachings and try to apply them to our own time and place. "Discipleship," Webb writes, "is the creative act of fitting our lives into his."[187] Vegetarianism is not required for Christians, "but it is a consequence of the Christian hope for a peaceable kingdom, where God will be all in all and all violence will come to an end."[188]

There was an early movement of Jewish followers of Jesus who opposed both sacrificing and eating animals. They were called the Ebionites ("the poor" in Hebrew). In their gospel, Jesus proclaims: "I came to do away with sacrifices, and if you don't stop sacrificing, you won't stop experiencing wrath."[189] Many scholars think that the Ebionites refrained from meat because they were concerned about spiritual purity. But Keith Akers, author of *The Lost Religion of Jesus*, thinks that the Ebionites' vegetarianism was an extension of their pacifism, something that was handed down to them from Jesus.[190] Their prospects for survival as a movement weren't good, since they distanced themselves from both conventional Judaism and the dominant Pauline style of Christianity. The Ebionites disappeared from history sometime during the fifth century.

All Food Is Clean

In Matthew's gospel, Jesus declares that "it is not what goes into the mouth that defiles a person, but it is what comes out of the mouth that defiles."[191] This saying has been interpreted by many Christians as a suspension of Jewish dietary laws, like the prohibition on eating pork. Mark thought so, adding to the end of his account of this teaching: "Thus he declared all foods clean."[192] Many contemporary Christians have cited this passage as evidence that meat-eating is morally acceptable. "Scriptures are clear," writes one American minister. "It is not wrong to eat bacon, or eggs, or steak or any red meat."[193]

But Bible scholar Jesper Svartvik doesn't think that Jesus intended to do away with Jewish dietary laws. He points out that in both Matthew's and Mark's gospels, this teaching comes right after Jesus accuses his opponents of abandoning "the commandment of God" in favor of "human tradition." Why then would Jesus himself "abandon the commandment of God" by encouraging people to eat food that violated mosaic laws?

Furthermore, there were many lively debates among early Christians about whether or not they should follow these laws. If Jesus had made a clear pronouncement on this topic, why didn't they refer to it?

Svartvik believes that Jesus was responding to "extremists" who wanted all Jews to follow the strict diet of the temple priests. Jesus challenged their puritanical approach and encouraged them to be more concerned about what "comes out of the mouth" – evil talk about others.[194]

If Svartvik is correct, Christians can't use this passage to claim that eating pork or other meat is acceptable in the eyes of Jesus. Jesus didn't simply do away with all standards. Consider the macabre example of cannibalism, which is said to have been practiced on several continents. If Jesus were indeed giving us the go ahead to consume anything edible, then even human flesh becomes legitimate food. We must ask the broader questions about how our food is produced. Was anyone harmed in the process? Vegetarianism is not about keeping the body "clean," but about refusing to contribute to violence.

Authoring Gospel

Books of the Bible often build off of each other. It can be useful to think of the Bible as a continuous act of interpretation. When we interpret the Bible today, we aren't doing anything radically different from the authors themselves. "Thus the interpreters become a link in the continuous chain of interpretation," writes Bible scholar Krister Stendahl, "this peculiar art of faithfulness and creativity that characterizes all living tradition."[195]

The divine mystery reveals itself also in our time. We who live today are just as privileged as Moses, Luke and Paul. God communicates no less with us now than in antiquity. With bold and fearless interpretation, we can discover new ways of living the gospel.

Macarius of Alexandria was a monk who lived in the Egyptian desert during the fourth century. One day, a hyena came to him, holding her pup in her mouth and weeping. The saint took the pup in his hand and saw that the little animal was blind in both eyes. He spat on its face and touched

its eyes with his fingers. Immediately, the pup could see. It ran straight
for its mother. This launched a long friendship between Macarius and the
hyena.[196] Saint Kentigern of Glasgow (d. ca. 603) healed a robin that some
boys had cruelly torn apart. Martin de Porres used his special abilities to
heal many animals, among them a donkey with a broken leg. After a man
had slaughtered a goose to make a pie, Saint Werburga of Chester (d. ca.
699) brought the animal back to life.[197]

The gospels testify to Jesus' solidarity with downtrodden people, but
nowhere does he heal birds or save hares from hunting parties – works of
mercy that are often undertaken by the saints. Still, we recognize Jesus in
the saints' commitment to animals. His ministry has been relocated to a
different social context. Something new has been created. The lives of the
saints are expressions of the "peculiar art of faithfulness and creativity"
that Stendahl calls for.

Bonaventure wrote that Saint Francis was once "offered a large fish
that was still alive. Calling it by name in his usual brotherly way, he put
it back in the water next to the boat."[198] He blessed the fish before they
parted ways. Bonaventure surely had never read of Jesus doing anything
similar on the Sea of Galilee, yet he didn't hesitate to describe Francis
both as an animal lover who possessed "the virtue that unites all creatures
in brotherhood," and as a "perfect" follower of Christ.[199]

We believe that every Christian and every Christian community has
this vocation: with their lives to write a new story about the God who
loves and liberates.

– 12 –
RELEASE TO THE CAPTIVES:
CHRISTIANS AND SLAVERY

A QUAKER SERVICE consists mainly of silence. The congregation waits in
the stillness for an address from God. At such a service in Burlington,
New Jersey, the silence was shattered when Benjamin Lay (1681–1759)
tramped into the meeting house, stopping in the center of the room. "You
slaveholders!" he shouted. "Why don't you throw off your Quaker coats
as I do mine, and show yourselves as you are?" He threw off his cloak and
stood in front of the astonished congregation in a military coat and with
a sword dangling from his hip. He drew his sword and held it in one hand,
in the other he held a large Bible. "In the sight of God you are as guilty
as if you stabbed your slaves to the heart, as I do this book!" Inside the
Bible was a bag of red dye. When he pierced it, the people around him
were splattered with what looked like blood.[200]

In 1737, Lay published *All Slave-keepers that keep the Innocent in
Bondage, Apostates* – one of the earliest anti-slavery texts of colonial
America. The book contrasts the brutality of slavery with the Christian
faith, which Lay writes is "so full of Mercy, Compassion, Forgiveness to
the very worst of Enemies, Tenderness, Meekness, Mildness, Sweetness
of love, and Pity to all Creatures of all kinds." This passage ends with a
reference to Proverbs: *"the merciful Man is merciful to his Beast."*[201] It
wasn't a coincidence, then, that Lay used pokeberry juice and not animal
blood during his dramatic protest in Burlington. He was a vegetarian and
didn't wear clothes made from skins of animals.

Lay's concern for animals and his criticism of slavery intertwined,
and he wasn't alone. "In the late eighteenth century many of the champi-
ons of animals were simultaneously active in other spheres," writes the
English historian Keith Thomas. "Usually ... the concern for animal wel-

fare was part of a much wider movement which involved the spread of humane feelings towards previously despised human beings, like the criminal, the insane or the enslaved."[202]

Englishmen Thomas Tryon (1634—1703), John Wesley (1703—91) and William Wilberforce (1759—1833) attacked slavery and advocated at the same time ethical treatment of animals.[203] The same was done by many on the other side of the Atlantic. Vegetarianism was part of what in the years before the Civil War was called "the Sisterhood of Reforms," one of the many issues – including temperance, abolitionism, women's rights – that many activists thought were interconnected and that ought to be engaged simultaneously.

David Cambell established a vegetarian boarding house at Oberlin College, one of the bulwarks of abolitionism in America.[204] Harriet Beecher Stowe (1811–96), author of *Uncle Tom's Cabin*, referred to transport cages for birds as "slave ships."[205]

The transcendentalist Amos Bronson Alcott – who was arrested for tax-refusal, an act of resistance against a government who tolerated slavery – wore canvas shoes since he considered leather to be "an invasion of the rights of animals." The pacifist abolitionist Henry Stephens Clubb fought – unarmed! – in the Civil War (he survived a bullet wound). He would later become the President of the American Vegetarian Society. The Quaker Valentine Nicholson – who housed runaway slaves in his home – abhorred violence to animals from an early age. After a hunt, he saw skinned animals for the first time. "It was repulsive and shocking to my young mind to see the bloody and bruised animals."[206]

The abolitionist-vegetarians horror at the killing of animals comes across clearly. Orson Johnson was shocked to find "the carcass of a DEAD HOG!!" while visiting a radical experimental farm in Indiana. Even worse – some of the pig was served for supper that same night.[207] "I'm tired of living among squealing hogs and squalling chickens and bawling cows and murdered calves and slaughtered lambs and barking dogs and where even the free birds of heaven hardly dare come near while chanting their sweet song," the Quaker schoolteacher Emily Gardner told friends. "The idea of taking the life of innocent animals always appeared so horrible that I abandoned the use of their flesh before I knew there was such a person in existence as [plant-food advocate] Sylvester Graham."[208]

Several utopian communities combined abolitionism, women's emancipation, education, vegetarianism, the sharing of possessions, and other social reforms. In the abolitionist newspaper *Regeneration* – published by a vegetarian anarchist – Marenda B. Randall described the meals at the Skaneateles Community in New York. "We all sit down together, to a purely vegetable diet. Very much do we enjoy our meals. At least I do, and the rest seem to."[209] Fruitlands was a short-lived community, established in 1843 in Harvard, Massachusetts by the visionary educator Amos Bronson Alcott and the English political philosopher Charles Lane. Eleven-year-old Anna Alcott – daughter of Bronson Alcott and the pioneering social worker Abigail May Alcott – expressed the community members' respect for animals. "We have power to think and feel with," she wrote, "and they have not the same power of thinking, they should be allowed to live in peace and not made to labour so hard and be eaten so much ... Besides flesh is not clean food, and when there is beautiful juicy fruits who can be a flesh-eater?"[210]

But animal abuse and human slavery have more in common than their opponents. They are structurally similar. They are upheld by some of the same ways of thinking, relying on the belief that domination and subjugation are the natural order of the universe. The Episcopal pastor Alexander Crummel, himself the son of a slave, said that slavery rests on "the disposition, on the part of the strong and selfish, to use and employ the weak and miserable part of creation as their own instruments."[211] In 1838, South Carolina senator William Harper gave this argument in favor of slavery: "It is as much in the order of nature that men should enslave each other, as that other animals should prey upon each other."[212] Animals eat each other, people say today, so why shouldn't we eat them?

Slave traders were white, but slaves were generally captured by fellow Africans. "As such, the slave trade was not a simple case of white oppression of black," writes Marjorie Spiegel in her book *The Dreaded Comparison*, "but of the powerful preying on the weak."[213] We can see this in our treatment of animals. John Twedell (1769–99), a Cambridge scholar, became a vegetarian after he was convinced that "we have no other right, than the right of the strongest, to sacrifice to our monstrous appetites the bodies of living things."[214]

Of course there are differences between animal abuse and slavery. Slave masters used psychological abuse to convince slaves that they were inferior, thereby internalizing their oppression. Animals can't suffer self-hatred in the same way.

Naturally, animals and humans have different needs. Something that is experienced as demeaning or painful for a human need not be for an animal. Cows can live contentedly on a square mile of pasture, but were humans forced to spend their entire lives confined to such a small area, they would feel like prisoners.

Animals can suffer in ways that adult humans cannot. Pigs on a factory farm can't make sense of their torment. They can't comfort themselves by planning a gruesome revenge, or in promises of a heavenly reward. "We live so little time in this world," wrote one Christian slave, "that it is no matter how wretched and miserable we are, if it prepares us for heaven."[215]

Another fundamental difference between humans and animals is that humans can learn from mistakes in the past to help us overcome the injustices of today. That is the purpose of this chapter.

Christians Defend Slavery

In the beginning, all people were equal. God introduced slavery, argued the early church father Augustine, as a punishment for human sin. Slavery is part of the new order that was established after the flood. People are obliged to follow the order of the fallen world, not the order of paradise.[216] This theology has its advocates today. They argue that God changed the rules after the flood, doing away with the plant-based diet of Eden. "This is God's law for today," writes one critic of animal rights, "rather than the laws He gave Adam and Eve in the garden. Those who say otherwise are the ones rebelling against God's laws."[217]

The Catholic Church followed Augustine's logic and defended slavery into the middle of the nineteenth century. In 1866, responding to the U.S. Emancipation Proclamation of 1863, the Vatican declared that slavery "is not at all contrary to the natural and divine law."[218]

Protestantism hasn't, on the whole, been fundamentally different. The Reformation didn't reform the church's view of slavery. A group of German serfs in 1525 demanded freedom with the argument that Christ had shed "His precious blood" for all humans, "the lowly as well as the great." Martin Luther sharply denounced their demand. "Did not Abraham [Gen. 17:23] and other patriarchs and prophets have slaves?" Their argument in favor of freedom "absolutely contradicts the gospel. It proposes robbery, for it suggests that every man should take his body away from his lord, even though his body is the lord's property."[219]

In February of 2002, Australian activists Patty Mark (then age 52) and Pam Clarke (then age 60) rescued eight sick hens from a factory farm. They were among 40,000 hens crowded into the farm, many of which were suffering from "overgrown claws, badly mutilated beaks, anemic combs and cloudy eyes." The next day the activists held a press conference to announce the rescue. The two women were arrested and later tried and convicted of burglary.[220]

Theological Arguments

Luther wrote that "a worldly kingdom cannot exist where there is no class distinction." This hierarchical understanding of society is ancient. The Greek philosopher Aristotle claimed that slavery was the order of nature. Intelligent beings had the right to dominate those they perceived to be inferior: free citizens over slaves; men over women; humans over animals. This thinking was adopted by the U.S. Senator William Harper, who argued that God ordered the world so that "the being of superior faculties and knowledge, and therefore of superior power, should control and dispose of those who are inferior."[221] As we've seen in an earlier chapter, the idea that creation is an intellectual pyramid – in which the reasonable can exploit the intellectually weak – has had a great impact on Western philosophy and theology. It has legitimized slavery. Today it legitimizes the oppression of animals.

Harper presented another argument for slavery that sounds familiar to modern day animal advocates. Slavery had always been around and therefore was "consecrated by the usage of generations."[222]

Some Christians didn't settle with defending slavery. They attacked abolitionists for denying the Bible,[223] being "self-righteous,"[224] and harboring hatred against God's laws.[225] They called them "fanatical and dangerous"[226] people who wanted to push "politics" into the church.[227] In 1864, the Southern Presbyterian Church declared that abolitionism was "unscriptural and fanatical ... one of the most pernicious heresies of modern times."[228]

Christian abolitionists were mocked for trying "to erect men a higher standard of morals than the Almighty has revealed, or our Saviour preached."[229] In 1850, a prominent Southern journal published a pro-slavery essay based on Paul the apostle's return of the runaway slave Onesimus. The author pointed out that Paul didn't criticize the slave master, nor did he "send him to some foreign country, whereby he might have escaped from oppression. But Paul sent him back. Our northern friends think that they manage these matters better than Paul did."[230] Senator Harper regarded as "sentimental" any discussion of equal rights, including the "inalienable rights" put forth by the US Declaration of Independence.[231]

The Lutheran theologian C. F. W. Walther (1811–87) dismissed the abolitionists as "anti-Gospel and anti-Christ."[232] They were well-meaning, but they had abandoned Christ for the "spirit of the times" – secular movements like humanism and philanthropy. Concepts such as "inherent human rights," he argued, were alien to Biblical Christianity.[233] The author and devout Christian Frederick Douglass (1817—95), himself a former slave, wrote that people often approached him after his anti-slavery lectures and asked: "Douglass, are you not afraid of injuring the cause of Christ? You do not desire to do so, we know; but are you not undermining religion?"[234]

Many of the arguments put forward by the apologists for slavery reappear in today's debates about the moral standing of animals. Animal rights advocates are called "self-righteous,"[235] their compassion "vain imagination and twisted sentimentality."[236] They are accused of secularism, New Ageism and "animal-worship."[237] They "hate and reject what God has to say about animals," and "represent one facet of a modern-day return to the paganism of the Ancient World."[238] In an article in *Christianity Today*, Charles Colson (former chief counsel for Richard Nixon) writes: "The philosophy behind the animal-rights agenda is an assault on human dignity." He called animal rights proponents "dangerous."[239]

More extreme charges have been leveled. In a lecture he delivered in 2000, the Italian Cardinal Giacomo Biffi said that the modern Antichrist was likely to be disguised as "an admirable philanthropist, a committed, active pacifist, a practicing vegetarian, a determined defender of animal rights."[240] Likewise, defenders of slavery accused abolitionists of satanic influence. Were the abolitionists doing the will of God? the former Governor of South Carolina, James Henry Hammond, asked in 1845. "No! God is not there. It is the work of Satan."[241]

Jesus, the Apologist

Moses Stuart (1780–1852) is widely considered to be the founder of Bible scholarship in the United States. In 1850, he published an extensive analysis of Bible passages that he believed supported slavery. He wrote that Jesus "doubtless felt that slavery might be made a very tolerable condition, nay, even a blessing to such as were shiftless and helpless, in case of kind and gentle mastership."[242]

In 1865, the Presbyterian minister Stuart Robinson argued that slavery was accepted in both testaments, and was supported by Paul. He warned that condemning slavery would deny that Scripture is inspired, thereby invalidating the entire Bible.[243]

Others pointed out that, while Jesus expressly did away with parts of the Mosaic Law – on polygamy and divorce, for example – he did nothing of the sort regarding slavery. It was only logical, then, to conclude that he had no objections to the order that God introduced after the Fall.[244] If Jesus had opposed slavery, he would have said so clearly, rather than leaving it up to his followers to figure out.[245]

In Mary Eastman's *Aunt Phillis's Cabin; or, Southern Life As It Is* (1852), she claimed that although the slaves could not have "escaped his all-seeing eye," the Son of God came not to give them liberty. "Oh! No; he came to redeem the world from the power of sin; his was no earthly mission; he did not interfere with the organization of society."[246]

Apologists for slavery had no difficulty finding Bible passages that supported their cause. "Who among you would say to your slave who has just come in from plowing or tending sheep in the field, 'Come here at once and take your place at the table'?" Jesus asks in Luke's gospel. "Would you not rather say to him, 'Prepare supper for me, put on your apron and serve me while I eat and drink; later you may eat and drink'?"[247] Jesus and his disciples were viewed as indifferent to the suffering of slaves. "Although Slavery in its revolting form was everywhere visible around them," wrote Senator James Henry Hammond in 1845, "no visionary notions of piety or philanthropy ever tempted them to gainsay the LAW, even to mitigate the cruel severity of the existing system."[248]

Today, many Christians use the same rationale to justify the abuse of animals. Jesus clearly cared more about human beings than animals – after all, didn't he eat the Passover lamb? If he hadn't accepted the killing of animals as the natural order of things, wouldn't he have said so? If Jesus were alive today, he surely wouldn't torment any animal unnecessarily, but to "mitigate the cruel severity of the existing system" of factory farming wouldn't be a priority for him.

Jesus, the Abolitionist

Scripture and tradition seemed to give slavery proponents the upper hand. Abolitionists responded with a more interpretive use of the Bible. They talked about the spirit and main features of Jesus' life and teachings. The "maxim widely prevails in the world," wrote the American reformer Beriah Green in 1839, "that it is the privilege, prerogative, and mark of greatness, TO EXACT SERVICE; that our superiority to others, while it authorizes us to relax the exertion of our own powers, gives us a fair title to the use of theirs; that 'might,' while it exempts us from serving, 'gives the right' to be served. The instructions of the Savior open the way to greatness for us in the opposite direction. Superiority to others, in whatever it may consist, gives us a claim to a wider field of exertion, and demands of us a larger amount of service."[249]

"Is not Jesus still the resurrection and the life?" asked Angelina Grimké (1805–79), abolitionist and daughter of a slaveholder. "Did He come to proclaim liberty to the captive, and the opening of the prison doors to them that are bound, in vain?"[250]

In 2001, an American animal rights organization distributed 20,000 Easter cards that asked the question "What Wouldn't Jesus Do?" The cover had an image of a serene Jesus standing next to a calf. On the inside, Jesus was wielding a bloody knife and slitting the calf's throat. The message read: "Jesus was the Prince of Peace, Not a Bloody Butcher! Go Vegetarian."[251] This strategy could have been taken from Grimké's 1836 *Appeal To The Christian Women of the South.* "Can you for a moment imagine the meek, the lowly, and compassionate Savior, *a slaveholder*?" she asks, "do you not shudder at this thought as much as at that of his being a *warrior*? But why, if slavery is not sinful?"

In the same year, Grimké's sister Sarah wrote *An Epistle to the Clergy of the Southern States* (1836), in which she claimed that slavery in America was far more brutal than it was in Biblical times. By the same token, some Christian vegetarians point out that today's animal agriculture is dramatically different than that of ancient Palestine. It is one thing to eat comparatively small amounts of meat from animals raised on the

79

land; quite another to gorge on the flesh of animals that have never seen the sunlight.[252]

A Gentle Revolution

In 1787, three out of every four people on earth were enslaved or in some sort of bondage. If you were to propose abolishing slavery, writes Adam Hochschild, author of *Bury The Chains: The British Struggle to Abolish Slavery* (2005), "nine out of ten people would have laughed you off as a crackpot. The 10th might have admitted that slavery was unpleasant but said that to end it would wreck the British Empire's economy."[253] Yet, that year a dozen people met in a bookstore in London to launch what Hochschild calls "one of the most far-reaching citizens' movements of all time": a campaign to end slavery in the British Empire. In only twenty years' time, the British parliament had outlawed the slave trade.

The next step was to abolish slavery altogether. In the 1830s, a new British campaign formed with that purpose. News of it gave hope to slaves in the British West Indies, who launched a massive revolt in Jamaica in 1831. Their revolt was crushed, but Hochschild believes that it was the decisive factor in convincing the British parliament to abolish all slavery in 1838.[254]

Here we see a radical difference between the oppression of humans and animals. The liberation of the latter can in no way be their own achievement. Animals are completely dependent on us. "When his own cup of suffering is full and overflowing, desperate resort to revolution sometimes rids him of his cruel tormentors and taskmasters," wrote the American abolitionist Julius Ames in 1835. "But of the inferior animals, generations and generations suffer and expire without any chance of relief or redress, unless it be granted by the generosity and justice of man."[255]

Resistance by slaves was of course fraught with risk, but free abolitionists also paid a heavy price. They were ridiculed and assaulted, lost their jobs and faced death threats. Those who helped people escape from slavery risked even more. One young minister who harbored hundreds of runaway slaves was caught and sentenced to six years of hard labor. He died in prison at the age of 33.[256] A South Carolina woman who hid two fugitive slave children was herself sold into slavery, along with her own children.[257]

Such heroism is not demanded of us today. To simply roll the shopping cart past the meat aisle of the grocery store and instead reach out for a bag of chickpeas – this is to join the long, humanizing tradition that the abolitionists were a part of and that today is carried on by, among others, the animal rights movement.

$-$ 13 $-$

O BREATH OF HOLINESS:
LIFE-GIVING SPIRITUALITY

BEFORE AFRICANS WERE FORCED onto slave ships bound for Portugal, Christian priests would sprinkle them with holy water as part of a baptismal ceremony.[258] Captain Sir John Hawkins, who initiated the British slave trade in the 1560s, offered twice-daily religious services for the crew of his ship "Jesus of Lübeck." The English slave trader John Newton (1725–1807) spent one to two hours each morning in prayer and Bible reflection.[259] Somehow these traditional expressions of Christianity – baptism, Eucharist, sermons, hymns, prayers, organ music, reverence for the saints – existed side by side with the enslavement of fellow human beings. We often think that spiritual exercises will help us become better Christians and lead us closer to God. But religious observance doesn't seem to have brought slavery apologists to see their captives as brothers and sisters. Why didn't God's spirit work more forcefully through the rites of the church? Perhaps the idols of money and prestige held too tight a grip on people.

Quakers do not baptize or celebrate the Eucharist. They have no programmed singing of hymns during services. They aren't interested in the rituals that other Christians consider helpful for their spiritual growth. Yet the members of this community have been comparatively insightful and forward-thinking. In the era of slavery, they demonstrated a level of spiritual discernment that many other Christian communities lacked. What does this say about the established holy rites? Nothing new, perhaps. The prophets of the Old Testament warned against undue focus on religious rites. In the book of Amos, God rebukes Israel:

> "I hate, I despise your religious feasts;
> I cannot stand your assemblies ...

Away with the noise of your songs!
I will not listen to the music of your harps.
But let justice roll on like a river,
righteousness like a never-failing stream!"[260]

But even Quakerism is no guarantee for clear-sightedness. Like other Quakers, the Friends Meeting of Burlington, New Jersey sat in silent worship and listened for God's will. Yet they didn't hear God speak about the unrighteousness of slavery. It was necessary for Benjamin Lay to barge in and proclaim it to them.

The Bulwark of Life

Many Christian communities have failed to defend the downtrodden. This is regrettable. After all, it should be the striving of all Christians to help the living remain living and live well. Such a life-affirming spirituality honors all the three persons of the Godhead. God the Creator is the origin of all life. Jesus said that he had come to give "life to the full." The Holy Spirit is the life-giver, "the life of life for all creatures," "the bulwark of life," "the liberator of the fettered" — to borrow words from a medieval prayer.[261] We encounter this spirituality in the American farmer and Quaker Joshua Evans (1731-98). "I thought I saw, and had to believe" he wrote, "that life was intended to be at the disposal of him who gave it." Evans often traveled to the homes of fellow Quakers and urged them to free their slaves. On such journeys, Evans lived on a simple diet of water, milk and bread. He notes in his journal that his strength and endurance matched that of any non-vegetarian. His diet grew out of a religious reverence for life: "as we cannot give life, let us be very cautious of taking it away... those who refuse to take life or partake of animal food can hardly be thought offensive to God and ought not to be censured or condemned by men."

Evans believed that his life shouldn't cause other living creatures to die. This humility was shared by Clara Barton (1821 — 1912), founder of the American Red Cross. Writing on her lack of desire for eating the flesh of animals, she explained that the "bountiful ground has always yielded enough for all my needs and wants."[262] Such an attitude makes it easier for the person who wants to develop a life-affirming spirituality. Evans and Barton have a sound appreciation of their place in the world, rooted in the understanding that all life belongs to God. We have no right to kill and enslave other beings.

"I considered that life was sweet in all living creatures," Evans reflected. Life *is* good, and we can act as agents of the spirit of life. In a society permeated with injustice, a life-affirming spirituality must be expressed in practical ways. The Holy Spirit is no theory. The spirit, "the bulwark of life," wants to be embodied in our lives.

Lasting Commitment

Many young people enthusiastically enlist in movements for social change – fighting for animal rights, saving the environment, confronting corporate globalization, ending homelessness, and so on. As the years go by, this commitment often wanes. We turn inward — toward our own education, careers and families. Some of the causes of this retreat from activism are reasonable. People who work full-time jobs and raise young children have little time and energy to spare for social causes. It can be difficult to find an organization that suits us – if we do, we might discover stressful conflict within the group, odd subcultures, and poorly functioning meetings. But the world needs our talents – even more so when we have gathered knowledge and life experience.

Maturity is a process of moving away from narrow self-interest, toward a deepening concern for the world and its inhabitants – particularly those in greatest need. We can't do everything, and we might need to focus on one campaign at a time. But the movement of our lives should be toward an ever-deepening compassion and commitment to love in action. For this, the modest farmer Joshua Evans appears as a spiritual guide: "my mind was enlarged in love of God and to my brethren, my neighbors and fellow creatures throughout the world."[263]

Sometimes the will to change our lives for the sake of others is abruptly awakened. It might happen when someone asks the church council to hide a refugee family that is threatened with deportation. It might happen when a high school student is informed by her teacher that her class will be dissecting frogs the next day. "O breath of holiness, fire of love, sweet taste for our soul!" Hildegard of Bingen exclaims in a song of praise to the Holy Spirit. "You fill our hearts with the sweet scent of the virtues."[264] To move from egoism to love has, throughout the centuries, been regarded as a sign of spiritual maturity. We must cherish those moments when our hearts are touched by the holy breath of compassion.

The Difficult Voyage

"Whoever does not love does not know God, for God is love."[265]

If we don't live in love, we distance ourselves from God. The Bible makes this clear in terms of relationships with our fellow human beings; but since God cares for all creatures, this truth applies also to our relationships with animals. Indifference to animals contributes to alienation between humans and God. This theological premise is the theme of "The Rime of the Ancient Mariner," Samuel Taylor Coleridge's (1772—1834) most famous poem.

Coleridge's mariner recounts a harrowing sea voyage to the South Pole. For awhile, an albatross follows the ship, winning the hearts of the crew:

> *And a good south wind sprung up behind;*
> *The Albatross did follow,*
> *And every day, for food or play,*
> *Came to the mariners' hollo!*[266]

But, without provocation, the mariner shoots and kills the bird. A curse descends on the ship, the sea burns, and a ghost ship appears. Before the mariner's eyes, the rest of the crew falls down dead.

> *I closed my lids, and kept them close,*
> *And the balls like pulses beat;*
> *For the sky and the sea, and the sea and the sky*
> *Lay like a load on my weary eye,*
> *And the dead were at my feet.*[267]

The mariner must endure the accusing gazes of his dead crew for seven days and seven nights. He watches with contempt the creatures of the sea, angry that they live while his men have died. But one night, the mariner looks overboard and sees "water-snakes" swimming in the moonlight. A "spring of love" gushes from his heart, and he blesses these small and lowly creatures. Only then is the curse lifted, and the ship steers him home.

Finding Peace

At the end of Coleridge's poem, the mariner comes to understand the lesson of his experience:

> *He prayeth well, who loveth well*
> *Both man and bird and beast.*
>
> *He prayeth best, who loveth best*
> *All things both great and small;*
> *For the dear God who loveth us*
> *He made and loveth all.*[268]

Our relationship with God is only as strong as our love for others. As long as the mariner despised or ignored the small and anonymous creatures of the sea, his heart was "dry as dust." Not until he saw them as they truly were – God's beloved creatures – could he pray. Without compassion there is no genuine devotion.

The poem's eerie scenes remind us that violence against other beings is a crime of cosmic proportions. We might think that we benefit from our exploitation of animals, but at what cost? The sin harms the sinner as well. "Until he extends the circle of his compassion to all living things, man will not himself find peace," warns Albert Schweitzer.[269]

A few years ago, our friend Helena was arrested after painting the words "everybody wants to live" in broad daylight on the wall of an animal research laboratory. We understand these words as more than a political slogan – they proclaim the truth that God is the origin of all life, the One who has filled all creatures with the will to live. This recognition is a foundation for a life-affirming spirituality. "I am life that wants to live," Schweitzer writes, "in the midst of life that wants to live."

− 14 −
KINDNESS TO ALL CREATURES:
THE MUSLIM JESUS

ANNIKA REMEMBERS: *During the summer of 2004 I lived in Hebron, a predominantly Muslim city on the Palestinian West Bank. One day a man named Falah invited me to meet his cat. He served me coffee under a tree. Before I left, he asked me to pick some mint from his kitchen garden for good luck. Among the plants were two bowls of water. "The water is for the birds," he explained. "If you treat animals well, you will be rewarded by God."*

Many Muslims believe that all good actions taken on behalf of animals will be rewarded by God. This theme is found in popular moral tales, especially those with their origin in Sufism – the mystical tradition of Islam.

In one of these stories, the ninth century saint Bayazid takes a day's journey to a faraway city, where he buys cardamom. When he returns home, he discovers ants living among the seeds. "I have carried the poor creatures away from their home," he thinks. He gets up and begins to walk back to the city to return the ants.[270]

In another, Rabi'a (d. 801) travels to the mountains where she is surrounded by wild goats and gazelles. A friend of the saint appears and the animals scatter. "Why did they make friends with you but flee from me?" he asks. "Well, you eat of their fat," she explains. "Why shouldn't they be in fear of you?"[271]

Perceiving the Divine

Rabi'a was not unique. On Indian and Persian miniatures, Sufi saints are often shown together with birds, lions and gazelles. "For the Muslim mystic, this close relationship with the animal world is not at all amazing," writes Sufi scholar Annemarie Schimmel, "since every creature praises God in its own voice and he who has purified his soul understands their praise and can join them."[272]

A Sufi's spiritual maturity allows the Sufi to hear and see *something different*. Where others notice only howling and yipping, the mystic perceives the animal's relationship with God. To hear, see – and not see – is the theme in a Sufi legend about King David. The story tells of an ant passing in front of David as he was in the sanctuary. David is about to toss the ant out when he hears the insect's voice calling him: "O David, what wantonness is this that you intend to inflict upon me? It is scarcely your task to lay hands upon me in God's own house!" David is upset and wonders: "O God, how should I deal with Your creatures?" A voice answers: "Make it your habit to act out of fear of God so that none has to suffer on your account! Do not locate the true source of creatures in their bodies! Look rather at the mystery of their creation! If we were to order an ant to come out of its black robe, so many indications of divine unity would radiate from its breast that the monotheists of the world would be put to shame."[273]

Images of Christ

This chapter introduces you to stories from the Islamic tradition about Muslim saints and about Jesus, who is an important prophet in that faith. There are good reasons for Christians to consider them. Reading these stories is an exercise in approaching that which is different. We in the Christian tradition haven't always been good at that. Even between our denominations there has often been little interest in understanding each other's interpretation of the faith. Theologian Werner Jeanrond writes that "the history of the Christian movement is, on the whole, not a good illustration of how to deal constructively with that which is different."[274] The decision-makers in the church have been quick to distinguish between "heresy" and "orthodoxy." Instead of letting many voices be heard, the right to interpret the Bible has been reserved for a limited number of church authorities: bishops, priests and theologians. But Jeanrond reminds us that diversity is important. We should welcome as great a variation as possible when it comes to reading and interpreting Scripture. Together we can learn more – from each other and with each other – about the historical, theological and spiritual dimensions of Biblical texts.[275] We also need each other when it comes to understanding the sometimes enigmatic Jesus. We benefit from listening to diverse voices. New insights into the person Jesus can be found in unexpected places.

Consider the following example. In England in the year 1615, the minister of a rural Christian parish delivered a condemnation of "the Turkish religion." As evidence of the profane nature of Islam, the minister relayed to his congregation a popular Muslim morality tale, in which "a woman that, traveling a long journey, should make water in her hand and give it her dog that fainted, to restore him." According to the tale God rewards the woman's deed by taking her up to heaven, he explained to his parishioners, who were expected to react with disgust.[276] If the congregation had been open to new perspectives about God, they might have heard something quite different in the sermon than the minister had intended. Was the Muslim woman in the tale in fact an example to Christians of what it means to be Christ for our neighbor?

And what about Ahmad Refa'i? One day he saw a dog being thrown out of a city because he was suspected of having leprosy. People must have been repulsed by the dog's filth, smell, and wounds. The Sufi master, however, carried the dog to a peaceful place and cared for him for forty days, against the objections of his disciples.[277] This is a story about Muslim compassion, but might it give us new perspectives on Jesus? Isn't it also a story of the healing that he embodies? Christ is the one who, with gentle hands, washes, anoints and dresses all wounds. In one Sufi story, Jesus shows extraordinary concern for his gray donkey. He explains to his disciples: "Nobility is no more than humble service to the Creator and kindness to all creatures."[278]

The Radically Different

In general, the Christian churches haven't been good at dealing with different religions or even dissidents within its own tradition. And neither have they been good at dealing with other creatures. The hens, the cows, the mink – they are in many ways different from us. They look different, they speak different languages, they appreciate other things than we do. That is a reason why we look down on them. To escape our prejudices about animals, we need each other's help. We must inspire and challenge one another.

In the Middle East, pigs have traditionally been viewed as unclean and repulsive animals. The Sufis tell a story about Jesus encountering a pig on the road. He astonishes the people around him by greeting the pig and saying "Pass in peace." [279]

– 15 –
CONVERSION:
THE JEWISH PROPHETIC TRADITION

PELLE REMEMBERS: *Helena and I would drive the hens to their new home. The others would stay at the farm to meet the police, employees and neighbors. Peter and Erica unfurled a beautifully painted banner with images of uncaged hens and the words* A Life in Freedom, *the name of our group.*

The police had already arrived when a car came to a screeching halt and the owner of the farm jumped out. Paul went toward him with an outstretched hand. "Hi, my name is Paul Josefsson. We liberated some battery-caged hens from here." That's all he had time to say before the owner directed a knee toward his groin.

I felt lost during the trial. My memories are vague: paintings hanging in heavy frames on the courtroom walls; Helena sitting straight in her chair and answering questions clearly; the suits of the lawyers; a full courtroom.

My lawyer sat to my left. As far as I remember, we contradicted each other. He tried to minimize what we had done at the same time as I tried to tell how nonviolent disobedience had contributed to making Sweden a better society. I talked about the struggles of the labor and free church movements against the unjust laws of their time, and how their disobedience brought us freedom of religion and the right to strike. The prosecutor sat on the other side of the courtroom and listened with an expressionless face. Perhaps my reasoning appeared irrelevant to him. When I stopped talking I got the feeling that my statement had been incoherent.

My eyes wandered over the paintings hanging on the other side of the room, painted in colors that floated together into a dark, formless mess. One scene I have, however, registered with clarity. At the end of the trial, the judge asked us if we would go on doing these rescues. Paul sat far-thest from the judge and so was the last to answer. "I am a Jew. I am glad for those who broke the law and helped Jews escape from the Nazis." The judges, who had been looking tired and slumped in their seats, suddenly sat up. "I am afraid of a society where people would rather obey the law than care for the needs of others. I will continue to fight for the animals as long as I have the strength."

The sun shone through the dirty windows. Paul's Star of David neck-lace glimmered against his chest.

Among the popular Christian legends of medieval Europe, several tell about hunters who underwent a conversion upon meeting their prey. Christ revealed himself to Saint Hubert of Liège (d. 727) through a cross in a stag's antlers. To both Saint Julian 'the Poor' and to Saint Eustace (d. 118), Christ spoke through a stag's mouth. "A revulsion from all killing, includ-ing the killing of animals, is expressly and dramatically set as the main theme of Julian's conversion," writes one historian.[280] In another legend, a man named Branchion is in pursuit of a deer when the animal slips into a cave. His hunting dogs will not cross the threshold, so Branchion enters the cave himself. Inside, he is surprised to meet a hermit who protects the deer and at the same time converts the hunter to Christ.[281]

We often think of conversion in the sense of a person changing one's beliefs. But Biblical conversion encompasses the whole person, not just one's intellect and consciousness. It's about turning around and walking in a new direction.[282] The prophets of the Bible call for a reorientation: Put away the old egoistic self! Change your lives and deeds![283] They help bring us to conversion, pointing us toward new life possibilities.

As we have seen, conversion can be a jolting experience: Voices from heaven! Stags who speak! But it also happens in more subtle ways. The German saint Benno (1010—1106) often walked about the fields and forests in silent prayer. One day, he passed a marsh that was home to a loud frog. Benno asked the frog to stop croaking so not to disturb his meditation. As the saint continued to walk, a passage from the book of Daniel came to his mind: "Bless the Lord, whales, and everything that moves in the waters, praise and glorify him forever! Bless the Lord, all animals wild and tame, praise and glorify him forever!" Afraid that "the singing of the frogs might perchance be more agreeable to God than his own praying," Benno commanded the frogs to "praise God in their accustomed fashion." Soon, "the air and the fields were vehement in their conversation."[284]

A frog's croaking? We might wonder how that could possibly compare to a human being's beautifully-formulated songs of praise. But our species is not necessarily more important in God's eyes than any other parts of creation. Why should we assume that our songs are sweeter to God than the croaking of God's little creatures?

Benno was struck with spiritual clarity. He understood that, in God's reign, the insignificant are no longer insignificant. What is more, he chose to act on this insight.

The French mystic and social critic Simone Weil (1909–43) wrote about the need to "empty ourselves of our false divinity, to deny ourselves, to give up being the center of the world …, to discern that all points in the world are equally centers and that the true center is outside the world."[285] This resonates with Jesus' words that those who want to follow him must "deny themselves."[286]

Homo sapiens' conversion with respect to animals is in one sense about denying ourselves. We must give up our imagined position at the center of everything. But this is not about an unhealthy self-denial. Both humans and animals can live good lives on this planet. Care for animals and care for people are not mutually exclusive. On the contrary, a world in which people express their love through vegetarianism would in many ways be a better world for all.

Today, most food animals are raised in crowded factory farming operations. The renowned Worldwatch Institute points out that the spread of factory farming has unleashed a host of ecological and human health problems on the world. Intensive confinement of animals leads to the spread of diseases such as Avian flu, and the overuse of antibiotics on farm animals has equally disastrous human health effects; factory farmed animals are fed a steady diet of dangerous chemicals (including arsenic, growth hormones and PCBs) that are consumed by humans and released into the environment; industrial animal agriculture is particularly energy and water intensive; and animal waste from factory farms ends up polluting the air, water and soil.[287]

Raising cattle causes more greenhouse gas emissions than driving cars, a fact that often surprises environmentally concerned people. According to the United Nations Food and Agriculture Organization's 2006 report *Livestock's Long Shadow*, the livestock generate more greenhouse gas emissions as measured in CO_2 equivalent – 18% – than all forms of transportation combined. Henning Steinfeld, senior author of the report, said, "Livestock are one of the most significant contributors to today's most serious environmental problems. Urgent action is required to remedy the situation." One quick and easy action anyone can do is to adopt, or at least move toward, a plant-based diet.

There are other reasons to adopt a plant-based diet. "Scientific data suggest positive relationships between a vegetarian diet and reduced risk for several chronic degenerative diseases and conditions," wrote the authors of the American Dietetic Association's 1997 position paper on vegetarian diets, "including obesity, coronary artery disease, hypertension, diabetes mellitus, and some types of cancer."

Spiritual leaders do not place themselves in the centre of the world; rather, they reach out toward others. The Jewish mystic Zusya of Annopol was described by his contemporaries as a person who served God in love. Among other things, he traveled the countryside collecting funds to ransom prisoners. On one such occasion, he stopped at an inn where he noticed that the owner was keeping caged birds. Seized by compassion, he said to himself: "Here you are, Zusya, walking your feet off to ransom prisoners. But what greater ransoming of prisoners can there be than to free these birds from their prison?"

He opened the cage and the birds flew to freedom. When the innkeeper saw what Zusya had done, he was furious. "You fool! How could you have the impudence to rob me of my birds and make worthless the good money I paid for them?" Zusya replied: "You have often read and repeated these words in the Psalms: 'His tender mercies are over all His works.'" The innkeeper beat Zusya and threw him out, but Zusya went away with peace of mind.[288] Zusya died in 1800. On his tombstone are the words: "turned many away from sin."

Self-Deception

We like to think that only other people are cruel to animals – other classes, other nations, other ethnic groups. In the mid-1800s, for example, the well-off members of the Royal Society for Prevention of Cruelty to Animals campaigned vigorously against bull-baiting and cock-fighting, "sports" enjoyed primarily by England's poor, while seemingly ignoring vivisection, pleasure hunting and other offenses of the upper class. In a letter to the organization dated July 26, 1868, the philosopher John Stuart Mill announced his intention to distance himself from the organization "while it is thought necessary or advisable to limit the Society's operations to the offenses committed by the uninfluential classes of society."[289]

While we think that cruelty is the domain of other people, we tend to believe that we ourselves are caring. This was expressed well by Senator Hubert Humphrey during May 1956 hearings in the US Congress on the "Humane Slaughtering of Livestock and Poultry Act." "We Americans are inherently a humane and compassionate people," he said. "I think it is one of our great and one of our truly sterling qualities. We abhor cruelty in any form. We dislike to see suffering, whether human or animals."[290]

We all want to be good people. But if we live in the illusion that we are caring friends of animals, no conversion to righteousness can take place. The Swedish activist Henrik Engström has described the psychology of self-delusion. "At the daycare where my daughter Alva goes, they sing a song about an elf that intervenes to save the life of a hare that is being chased by hunters. It's thought-provoking that our society puts into children's heads that they should love and care for animals. The first present that children get is often a stuffed animal; there are pictures of animals on children's strollers, everywhere. Even the individuality of animals is brought out for children, as in the song about the elf and the hare. But you get the feeling that something shady is going on. Children and the rest of us are reared to believe that we all love animals. A good way of hiding oppression is to encourage people to delude themselves. To take the step from our image of ourselves as people who love and sympathize with animals to see that there is a systematic and brutal oppression of animals – and that we're part of it – is difficult, perhaps impossible."[291]

The Old Testament prophets told uncomfortable truths. Jeremiah criticized those who claimed that all is well: "'Peace, peace' they say, when there is no peace."[292]

Some people argue that it's possible to both care for animals and kill them. Industries that exploit animals claim this in their public relations material. "The technologies used by today's farmers provide the most comfortable living conditions that food animals have ever had," reads a March 2004 press release issued by the US agribusiness industry.[293] The website of the large pharmaceutical company Astra Zeneca declares that the company has "the greatest concern... for the health and quality of life of the animals" used in medical experiments.[294] Arla Foods, the largest dairy producer in Scandinavia, assures its customers that "the animals' comfort and well being is a priority."[295]

But these companies are abusing language. "Imagine the following," writes Henrik Engström. "I look after my neighbor's cat with the promise that the cat will 'be well cared for.' Upon coming home, the neighbor finds the cat killed and skinned. Of course I would be branded a liar. Why? Because 'well cared for' is not consistent with me intentionally harming the cat. If someone promises 'the greatest concern' and 'care,' that's exactly what we ought to expect."

The Rebirth of Hertz Grein

"HIS TENDER MERCIES are over all His works."

When Hertz Grein – the protagonist of Isaac Bashevis Singer's (1903—91) novel *Shadows on the Hudson* – hears these words in a synagogue, he asks himself: "Was God really good to all? Had He been good to the six million Jews in Europe? Was He good to all the oxen and pigs and chickens that people were slaughtering at this very moment?"[297] Grein stops reciting the liturgy and wants to tear off his prayer shawl.

Grein cheats on his wife, but decides to set his life on a better course. He returns to his Jewish faith, which – as he sees it – is based on the premise that "people should live in such a way that they did not build their happiness on the misfortunes of others." This leads him to adopt a vegetarian diet. "How could one serve God when one butchered God's creatures? How could one expect mercy from heaven when one spilled blood every day, dragged God's creatures to the slaughterhouse, caused them terrible suffering, shortened their days and years? How could one ask compassion of God when one plucked a fish from the river and looked on while it suffocated, jerking on the hook?"[298]

It shouldn't come as a surprise that a person's spiritual rebirth results in vegetarianism. As another of Singer's characters – the gentle professor Vladislav Eibeschutz – says, "There is no better way to serve the Creator than to be kind to His creatures."[299]

LIVE AND LET LIVE

PELLE REMEMBERS: *The line into the kitchen started in the corridor and moved slowly forward. Sleepily, I took the tray and pushed it along the counter. That day I noticed an unusual number of deep metal dishes marked with the letter "V."*

"Another one has arrived," said the man in the apron.

My first thought was that one of my activist friends had come here. But there hadn't been a trial recently, so that would have been impossible. Then who could it be? Maybe someone who was arrested during the riots at the EU summit? I peered around in the cafeteria to see if he would stand out. Maybe dreadlocks, or a skinny, pale figure with glasses. But there was just the usual crowd. Tom, with his goatee and the blue-green tattoos on his forearms. Lars, who bent forward as he ate, the muscles of his back bulging. His buddy Rickard sat as usual next to him in his white cross-training pants.

Life behind bars wasn't that bad. My sentence had generated some media publicity and I had given several interviews from prison. They were opportunities to explain why I believe it is necessary to stand up for oppressed animals. Several of the guards were quite sympathetic to my cause. One of them, a slender man in his twenties, announced one day that he'd stopped eating eggs from factory farms, and some time later that he'd stopped eating eggs completely. During day-time I sat at my little desk, reading my university course literature on New Testament studies.

That evening I was alone in the gym. I was cycling when a large, dark-skinned man entered. I hadn't seen him before. We greeted cautiously. He had strong shoulders and walked slightly stooped, with heavy steps. With a barbell in each hand, he sat down on a bench. A commercial radio station played pop music in the background.

"Are you a vegetarian?" he asked in good Swedish, but with a marked accent.

"Yeah."

"Me, too," he said. "For a month now. I hope it goes well."

He had been arrested smuggling goods from Norway to Sweden. Rice, cheese and other things, he said. His face was smooth, like a child, and there was something sad about it. He was Iraqi, supported the US invasion, but had a family in Baghdad.

"Bombings. Sure, I'm worried," he said. "But it's necessary to get rid of Saddam."

I didn't want to discuss the war with him. "And why did you become a vegetarian?" I asked as I pedaled, now at a slower pace.

"I have worked as a butcher. In Iraq, also in Sweden. They know. They have feelings. The animals know what will happen when they come for slaughter."

It isn't easy to convince people to kill other people. It takes time and training to get soldiers to break their entrenched objections to taking another human life. Militaries use many methods to cultivate the raw, brutal and violent within a soldier. Through propaganda, the enemy is deprived of their humanity. They are portrayed as "fanatics," "evildoers," "animals," "cockroaches." The fact that the military can refer to religious and moral authorities to support the killing helps break down any ethical reservations a soldier might have.

The instinctive revulsion to killing can also appear in situations where the victim is an animal. While working on this book in 2004, Pelle overheard a radio interview with a deer hunter. The woman recalled one of her first hunting memories. She was at her hunting stand when a doe with two fawns approached from the edge of the woods. Her heart raced as the animals walked across the field toward her. The animals came nearer and she readied to fire. The deer heard the click of the gun's safety mechanism, however, and ran back into the woods.

"I didn't fire a shot. At the same time, when you're new you have mixed feelings. I was relieved at the same time that I was disappointed."

"Why was it a relief?" asked the interviewer.

"It goes against the grain a bit to shoot when you aren't accustomed to it. You have a little psychological barrier that you need to overcome. The first time I fired a rifle my heart was racing. After that I could shoot sometimes. But then, suddenly, a situation can come up where you think, well, it's so beautiful around you and you don't want to shoot. You rather enjoy looking at the animal."[300]

In medieval paintings, hell is often portrayed as a place where the human-animal relationship is reversed: animals hunt, kill, and eat humans. Historian Boria Sax thinks that these paintings illustrate the doubts that people have always harbored about the morality of their routine violence against animals.[301]

We find testimony of these doubts from people in various epochs. The Irish philosopher Francis Hutcheson (1694–1746) wrote that slaughtering animals for food was "so opposite the natural compassion of the human heart" that it could only be justified by referring to Scripture.[302]

In an 1892 essay, the Russian novelist Leo Tolstoy wrote about meeting a butcher on the way to Túla, Tolstoy's hometown. "I asked him whether he did not feel sorry for the animals that he killed. He gave me the usual answer: 'why should I feel sorry? It is necessary.' But when I told him that eating flesh is not necessary, but is only a luxury, he agreed; and then he admitted that he was sorry for the animals. 'But what can I do?' he said, 'I must earn my bread. At first I was *afraid* to kill. My father, he never even killed a chicken in all his life.'"

In the same essay, Tolstoy gave an account of a conversation he had with another butcher, a retired soldier. He was "surprised at my assertion that it was a pity to kill and said the usual things about it being ordained. But afterwards he agreed with me: 'Especially when they are quiet, tame cattle. They come, poor things! trusting you. It is very pitiful.'"[303]

Genesis describes the first sin as Adam and Eve's disobedience of God's command to not eat "of the tree of knowledge of good and evil" (2:17). Perhaps, having eaten of this tree, they believed that they, rather than God, could determine good and evil. Rather than abide by God's plan for a harmonious world, they felt entitled to abide by the dictates of their own desires. It became tempting to kill animals for their flesh and skins. Two famous novels posit that violence against animals has been the first step in humanity's fall into violence and destructiveness. In Milan Kundera's *The Unbearable Lightness of Being* (1984), we read: "Mankind's true moral test, its fundamental test (which lies deeply from view), consists of its attitude towards those who are at its mercy: animals. And in this respect mankind has suffered a fundamental débâcle, a débâcle so fundamental that all others stem from it."[304]

In *Lord of the Flies* (1954) by Nobel Prize-winning author William Golding, a group of boys are deserted on an island. Once they overcome their reluctance to kill the wild pigs that inhabit the island, they go on to hunt and kill each other.

We were called to show compassion and mercy, yet humanity has chosen to kill other creatures. Does our reluctance to kill animals stem from our subconscious recognition that it is a rebellion against God's design for creation?

The Hidden Slaughter

As anti-slavery sentiment burgeoned in late-eighteenth century England, slave traders and owners responded with a concerted public relations campaign. It included the distribution of 8,000 pro-slavery pamphlets. The pamphlets described enslaved families living contentedly in "a snug little house and garden, and plenty of pigs and poultry."[305]

Two centuries later, a similar campaign of misinformation was conducted by Perdue Farms, one of the largest chicken factory farming operations in the United States. "Perdue chickens lead such a soft life that they can't help but turn out tender," read a Perdue newspaper ad. "They live in $60,000 houses, get eight hours' sleep and eat princely meals that include cookies for dessert!" The ad went on to say that on Perdue farms there is "no overcrowding" and that "every bird has plenty of room to roam."[306]

But the truth that animal advocates were uncovering about life on Perdue's factory farms was quite different than the picture presented in these ads. Perdue chickens were crowded – as many as 25,000 at a time – into windowless sheds. Each bird had one square foot or less of living space for its entire life. Disease, cannibalism and sudden death were byproducts of this overcrowding.[307]

Misrepresenting the living conditions of farm animals is a tactic that has been used over and over again to defend otherwise indefensible practices. But there are other ways of influencing public opinion. For instance, when the largest Swedish newspaper planned to publish a slaughterhouse exposé complete with color photographs, a representative of a large meat-producing company made a personal visit to the newsroom. The material was accurate, he admitted, but too graphic. People might stop eating meat, which would have serious economic consequences. He begged them not to run the story. The editor-in-chief responded by removing large sections of the text as well as the most gruesome photographs, and ordered all color photographs converted into black and white. How did the editor explain her actions? "If we accept that people have meat at the dinner table, we can't let them read these sorts of things over breakfast."[308]

In the United States, legislators in both Texas and Missouri have considered banning all photography inside slaughterhouses and factory farms, and assessing heavy fines on violators.[309]

Strong economic forces want us to close our eyes to what is happening to animals. How do we avoid being influenced by this? Bruce Friedrich, a Catholic activist who works with People for the Ethical Treatment of Animals, asks us to fight the temptation to distance ourselves from the brutal reality of the animal industry. It is morally incongruous to ask another person to do the dirty work for us. We should all ask ourselves whether we could, in good conscience, take part in de-beaking chickens, castrating cows without anesthetics, or working a commercial fishing trawler. "You know," writes Friedrich, "most of us could watch grains being tilled or even spend an afternoon shucking corn or picking beans, fruits, or vegetables. Seriously, how many of us would want to spend an afternoon slitting open animals' throats?"[310]

"More Compassionate Than the Almighty"

ANNIKA REMEMBERS: *In the early 1980s, my sister and I watched a TV documentary about the treatment of animals in factory farms. In one scene, you could see a calf standing in a narrow crate, unable to move. I was fourteen years old, my sister was twelve, and this film hit us in the gut. Why hadn't we been told about this earlier? How could people support this cruelty? We lay on the bed in mom's room and cried. She tried to answer our questions. She was probably unprepared for our strong reaction. That night, Gunilla and I made our decision. We were never going to eat meat again.*

We shouldn't idealize children's relationships with animals. Children can be cruel. Many children go through stages of development when they engage in violence – even torture – against insects and animals: pulling wings off of flies, shooting birds with BB guns, catching and beating snakes.[311] But children can also share a special affinity with animals. Augustine cited this as an example of children's poor judgment.[312] In an interview, Isaac Bashevis Singer said about his childhood: "you cannot be for justice while you take a creature which is weaker than you and slaughter it, and torture it. I've had this feeling since I was a child and many children have it. But somehow my parents told me that this means that I am trying to have more compassion than the Almighty. My mother told me that if I become a vegetarian I will die from hunger, from malnutrition. So I was afraid, I said, 'Well, what can I do?'"[313]

Singer's parents were doing what they thought was best for their children. After all, if there were vegetarian role models in early twentieth-century Poland, we can't imagine that they were accessible to a family living in a poor quarter of Warsaw.

An adult needs to be humble enough to take moral guidance from children. Mary Lou Randour shares a story of a mother who was introduced to the animal rights movement through her daughters – ages seven and nine. After the girls announced that they were becoming vegetarian, the mother "tried to encourage them to continue eating meat– but not for long. Listening more carefully, she began to join them in their thinking. They all began to read more about vegetarianism, which led them to learn about the condition and treatment of animals in modern society. Mother and daughters learned together, and they committed as a family to honoring life." [314]

The Swedish Quaker and pacifist Erik Kallesson was born in a working-class home in the 1910s. "As early as seven or eight I remember not eating meat," Kalleson recalled. "One time at that age I was with my father at my grandmother's. She had fried potatoes and pork. I can see the picture before me when she takes the frying pan and puts the potato and piece of pork on my father's plate, and a potato and piece of pork on my plate. Then I take my piece of pork and put it on father's plate. When grandmother catches sight of this, she says: 'No, the boy should have the pork!' 'The boy doesn't eat pork,' father then says. That is the first time that I remember that I didn't eat meat and flesh, and that the others had accepted it. My food in those days didn't amount to much. There weren't many vegetables in the working class homes of that time, and I was probably a bit undernourished. But vegetarianism has since then followed me throughout my life." [315]

It's easier to live as a vegetarian in northern climes today than in the 1910s. The shelves and frozen food aisles of grocery stores hold a wide variety of vegetarian food. Vegetarian children can grow up healthy on a meatless diet.

Let's take the challenge of children like the boy Kallesson seriously. Sometimes our children are God's agents of change.

"The Ox Fell, I Fell Too"

"It was so strange when I was a child," Kallesson wrote, "that when I saw a piece of meat or a meatball, I kind of saw the living animal in front of me, and it was impossible to get it down." [316] As a child, Kallesson had the gift of mystics and prophets: the ability to see the truth, beyond what lies in front of us. The truth about the meat is that someone was killed for it.

When Clara Barton was a young girl, she saw a group of farmhands butchering an ox. "One of the men carried an axe," she wrote in her auto-biography, "and stepping a little to the side and back, raised it high in the air and brought it down with a terrible blow. The ox fell, I fell too." When she awoke, she found herself lying in bed, her doting family at her side. They asked her what caused her to fall. "Someone struck me," she replied.[317] The experience had a lasting impact: "I lost all desire for meat, if I had ever had it – and all through life to the present, have only eaten it when I must for the sake of appearance, or as circumstances seemed to make it the more proper thing to do."[318]

How can we learn to identify with animals as the young Barton and the young Kallesson did? Austrian writer and pacifist Bertha von Suttner (1843–1914) answers: "in every living creature see yourself."[319]

— 17 —
UNLOVABLE ANIMALS

THE LATE SUMMER EVENING is warm, so we open the kitchen window. We're sitting and reading when a crane fly frees itself from the blackness of the August night and flies lazily past the kitchen table and up toward the light fixture. "A mosquito eater!" We stiffen a bit, lose our concentration, look up from our magazines. The fly buzzes as it dances around, bouncing on and off the light bulb. Then he tears himself loose and orbits, spiraling closer and closer to us! We leap up from our chairs with a shout and find refuge in the hallway. Is it the long legs that induce fear? They're sprawling under the fly. You don't want those in your face.

We calm down. He sits still. We trap him with a glass and sheet of paper, release him on the balcony and quickly close the door.

Human prejudices can cost animals dearly. How much of our indifference toward the oppression of pigs stems from our view of them as ugly, stupid and dirty? People who study animal behavior point out that the pigs are actually "cleanly, social and very quick to learn."[320] But that knowledge hasn't trickled down to the popular consciousness. Think of expressions such as "pig out" (overeat), "pig sty" (messy room), "pig-headed" (being stubborn beyond reason), or "piggish" (being dirty or unpleasant).

Rats are commonly used in laboratory experiments, in part because they are small and inexpensive. Another reason is that people don't feel sympathy for them – they have become a symbol of filth, disease and dishonesty. One dictionary refers to rats as "destructive pests."[321] Another gives two examples for the use of the word: "a large, disgusting rat snuck across the road," and – not coincidentally – "medical experiments with white rats."[322] "Rat" is often used as a slang term for a "despicable person," or "scab laborer."[323] Nazi propaganda likened Jews to rats; once a group of people is established as rat-like, it is easier to hate them. There are some historical explanations for our feelings about rats. In the countryside, they once competed with humans for scarce food resources; in the cities, they contributed to the spread of disease. But maturity requires that we widen our moral horizons and rid ourselves of prejudices that legitimize violence. For help, we can look to the examples of Jesus and the saints.

In one shocking Sufi story, Jesus and his disciples come across the corpse of a dog. The disciples complain about the stench, but Jesus corrects them: "Say nothing about God's creatures, except that which is in praise."[324] In another version of the story, Jesus says of the reeking corpse: "How beautiful are those teeth, displayed in the jaws!"[325] This is especially striking in light of the disdain in which dogs were held in classical Muslim culture.[326]

Christian spiritual masters remind us that no one of God's creatures deserves our disdain. The seventh century mystic Isaac the Syrian prayed for the reptiles – animals that rarely are the object of human affection.[327] Saint Silouan the Athonite (1866–1938), an uneducated Russian peasant who was canonized in 1988, described how he once saw a dead snake that had been cut into pieces, but was still writhing: "and I was filled with pity for every living creature, every suffering thing in creation, and I wept bitterly before God."[328] The compassionate French clergyman Jean Meslier (1664–1729) suffered when people stepped on spiders.[329]

This attitude finds its roots in Scripture. The author of the book of Wisdom writes of God's love for all of creation: "nothing that you have made disgusts you."[330] And what about worms? Surely they are unworthy. Not at all, explains a medieval Christian treatise, God "cares even for the worms."[331]

Beyond Warm Feelings

Cute animals enrich our lives. A puppy can bring out feelings of tenderness in people that they didn't know they had. But all animals are words of God, not only the cute ones. Every creature is an opportunity to express empathy and compassion.

Must we have warm feelings for all animals? To sympathize with rats who are running around in the attic – or a snake slithering toward you in the grass – is not easy. Secular animal rights philosophers have often emphasized that our moral obligations to animals do not depend on warm feelings. In a play published in 1895 by the *Vegetarian Review*, pioneering animal advocate Henry Salt opined that "if we are to fight vivisection, we must rid ourselves of this false 'love of animals,' this pampering of pets and lap-dogs by people who care nothing for the real welfare of animals, or even for the welfare of men."[332] Contemporary philosophers such as Peter Singer and Tom Regan argue that reason and logic – rather than emotion – should compel us to the cause of animals. This approach is different than what we take as a starting point in this book: Christian love. But they have something in common. For a Christian, love means seeing and responding to another's needs, not just warm feelings.

The Golden Rule

"In everything do to others as you would have them do to you," Jesus said.[333] This has come to be called the golden rule. As one writer points out, Jesus' teaching "is intended to shatter the radical self-centeredness that obscures our awareness of the rights and needs of others."[334] The golden rule does not demand that we harbor any particular emotional connection to others: it does not state what we are to *feel* for others, but what we are to do.

In 1776, the English doctor of divinity Humphrey Primatt expressed the same idea: "Do you that *are* a man so treat your horse, as you would be willing to be treated by your master, *in case* that you were a horse?"[335] The Danish priest Laurids Smith claimed in 1791 that the golden rule should also be applied in our relationship with animals, since animals also have needs. He wrote that humans ought to "towards the Animals observe justice" as we do with each other.[336] The American author Herman

Daggett – writing in the same year from the other side of the Atlantic – argued that Jesus' teaching "must extend to all sensible beings, with whom we have any dealings, and in whose situation we are capable of imagining ourselves to be."[337] In this way, Primatt, Smith and Daggett echoed the earlier works of the English social reformer and vegetarian Thomas Tryon (1634—1703), who claimed that animals bore the image of their Creator within themselves, and therefore had the right to concern and respect in the spirit of the golden rule: "do unto all creatures, as they would be done unto."[338]

Few of us apply the golden rule in our relationship with oppressed animals. It may be because of lack of interest, or lack of knowledge. In order to practice the golden rule, we must be aware of other's needs. On this point, science can come to our aid. Studies have shown that fish can feel pain. They have similar brains and nervous systems as other vertebrates. A fish's mouth is particularly sensitive – it is used to examine and collect things, much the same way as we use our fingers. Even if we don't know exactly how a fish feels when pierced by a hook and yanked out of the water, it must be painful. Humans tend to have as little sympathy for pike and perch as they do for rats and snakes. But the golden rule can be applied to them all, with the help of empathy and knowledge.

— 18 —
VEGETARIAN EUCHARIST:
ON CONTEMPLATIVE EATING

FROM THE BEGINNING of the Christian movement, social justice has been understood as a central element of the Eucharist. "You have tasted the Blood of the Lord, yet you do not recognize your brother," preached John Chrysostom, who served as Archbishop of Constantinople at the turn of the fourth century. "You dishonor this table when you do not judge worthy of sharing your food someone judged worthy to take part in this meal." [339] This theme is picked up in the Catechism of the Catholic Church, which explains: "The Eucharist commits us to the poor. To receive in truth the Body and Blood of Christ given up for us, we must recognize Christ in the poorest, his brethren." [340]

From a Biblical perspective, justice is part of a broader concept: *shalom*. The Hebrew word signifies a state of peace and wholeness. Where *shalom* is present, relations are right: between humans, between humans and animals, between creation and God. Everything is in harmony.

Animals are almost always absent from Christian reflection on the Eucharist. Even those who want to bring justice to the forefront as a theme in the Eucharistic rite normally limit it to concern for members of our own species. When this is done, God is made smaller than God is. We would like to see more examples of a Eucharistic theology which highlights human and animal relationships. The Lord's Supper is a powerful symbol for God's *shalom*. It consists of bread and wine, it is thus a peaceful meal. It is not founded in violence. For it to be prepared, no pig has to be driven into the slaughterhouse.

Daily Bread for Animals

In the early church, the Eucharist was part of a regular meal in which people ate until they were satisfied. Nowadays, the worshipper takes only a small peace of bread and a sip of wine. Even if it isn't a full meal, part of the meaning of the Eucharist is that we share the daily need for food with each other. The saints remind us that animals also have these needs. They have a right to their "daily bread"; to satisfy their hunger and thirst. The desert monk Macarius of Alexandria regularly provided a hyena with a loaf of bread, so the hyena wouldn't go hungry.[341] Many legends of the saints tell similar stories.[342]

In Dostoyevsky's novel *The Brothers Karamazov*, the monk Zosima recounts a story about Saint Sergius of Radonezh (1313–92), the patron saint of Russia. Sergius lived in the forest as a hermit. One day a bear came to his little hermitage "and the great saint felt tenderness for him, fearlessly went out to him and gave him a piece of bread, as if to say: 'Go, and Christ be with you.' And the fierce beast went away obediently and meekly without doing any harm."[343] This is a Eucharistic meal: bread shared, blessing given. The story of Saint Sergius' communion with the bear is a lens through which animals appear in a new light: no longer as resources at our disposal, but as brothers and sisters in Christ.

A Lutheran liturgical handbook from 2003 says that the Eucharistic bread left over from mass can be crumbled and given to birds in the church yard.[344] What a beautiful act. In a real way, the sparrows get a taste of how humans commune with the Creator.

We aren't proposing that animals should be invited into our churches on a regular basis. Our rites would probably not be meaningful for them. They have no need for such sacraments, since their relationship with God has not been corrupted. Humans — not animals — need spiritual healing. There is, however, a form of bread-breaking that is relevant to animals. When we humans share the earth's resources with them, we together celebrate the all-encompassing, universal Eucharist.

Choices of the Heart

The word "contemplation" comes from the Latin *contemplor*, to observe or to gaze attentively. Those who want to become contemplative wish to become aware of God's presence; they want to perceive God's redeeming participation in the world. Contemplation and attentiveness are connected. Animals have everything to win if we become more attentive to what kind of food we put in our mouths.

Mary Lou Randour tells the story of a woman named Carey, who returned to vegetarianism as part of a decision to deepen her Christian spirituality. The aroma of a grilling hamburger, or a turkey roasting in an oven, can make her mouth water. But she consciously brings an image to her mind of the animal who has suffered and died for the food that her stomach craves. By turning inward, to the will of the heart, she makes her decision. "I choose from my best self – my spiritual self," Carey explains. "I choose not to eat meat to honor the value of the creatures whose worth is equal to my own." Randour reflects: "Each time Carey decides what to eat, she develops her capacity to listen with her heart and to act out of generosity of spirit rather than from a narrow, fleeting self-interest."[345]

How can we follow Carey's example and become conscious of what we eat? Many Christians begin each meal with a song, prayer of thanksgiving, or a few moments of silence. These times are opportunities to offer thanksgiving for God's overflowing care, and to remember how good it is that no one has been killed for our dinner.

In the Roman Catholic tradition, the *Liturgy of the Hours* provides the faithful with a daily regimen of prayer and reflection, based largely on the Psalms. The prayer that it offers before a noon meal quotes from Psalm 145, a reminder that God is the good parent who looks after all of creation:

> *All look to you in hope*
> *and you feed them with the food of the season.*
> *And, with generous hand,*
> *you satisfy the desires of every living creature*[346]

Sacrifice

A radio journalist was touring a Swedish egg factory with a representative of the egg industry. The journalist noticed that the owner of the farm wore a protective mask when he entered the shed. He asked the representative if the hens shouldn't be wearing them, also. "We have to put higher priority on the human life than on the animal in this situation," the man replied. "A person that walks in there should wear a mask. This dust isn't good to get in your lungs, that's for sure."[347] The egg factory owner was willing to sacrifice the hens, but not himself.

In the Eucharist, we celebrate our communion with Jesus and remember the death that was a consequence of his self-giving love. Jesus chose to sacrifice himself, not someone else. The only legitimate sacrifice is the one that is self-chosen.

From Weapons to Tools of Life

ANNIKA REMEMBERS: *It was Christmas Eve in Risley. We had been locked into our cells for the night, and I had put my Christmas presents in front of me on the bed. Only one of them had managed to get through the censors without losing its wrapping paper. My evening snack – a cup of hot cocoa and mince pie – was sitting on the bedside table. I started my little Christmas celebration by praying for awhile for my mother, father, sister and friends. Then I tore into my presents.*

The atmosphere had been volatile on the cellblock that day. A drug raid made the morning chaotic, with accusations, anger, distrust, police dogs and transfers of prisoners. Four women left the cellblock, their few belongings in a plastic bag in their hands. Another four women had been transferred for other reasons or released, so we had eight new inmates.

During the evening mass, Father Richards and his assistant did their best to create a devotional mood. Some of the women couldn't take the silence and kept giggling. Father Richard became irritated. He asked one of the guards to lead them out and apologized to the rest of us when the mass was over. Well, well, I thought, it isn't easy. They had probably been in lockdown for most of the day.

So it was evening and I had my own little Christmas celebration. It was quiet in the prison other than sporadic banging against the wall by someone in the isolation unit.

The night of September 13, 1998, Annika – together with Ann-Britt Sternfeldt and Stellan Vinthagen – climbed the security fence of a nuclear submarine wharf in Barrow, England. The three plowshares activists non-violently dismantled a platform on the wharf. They then walked, household hammers in hand, toward the submarine under construction, with the intent of disarming it. However, before they could reach the construction site, security personnel arrested them. The activists were charged with "conspiracy to commit criminal damage", and they spent six months in prison.

The plowshares movement takes its name from the metal tip of a plow that cuts the earth. The Hebrew prophets Micah and Isaiah wrote about a time when humans "will beat their swords into plowshares and their spears into pruning hooks."[348] Plowshares activists try to apply this vision by hammering on, or dismantling weapons so that they can no longer be used to kill.

The prophet Micah describes a future where nations shall not train for war and where "every man will sit under his own vine and under his own fig tree, and no one will make them afraid."[349] Plowshares, pruning hooks, fig trees. These vegetarian symbols are consistent with the prophetic visions of humans and animals once again living in peace.

The Christian pacifist Leo Tolstoy (1829–1910) interwove these Biblical themes in his life and teaching. He had no doubt as to what God calls us: to build true justice and cooperation, and work to end strife and discord between and among people and other beings. This work, he explained, "is the realization of what the Jewish prophets promised, saying that the time will come when all men shall be taught the truth, when the spears shall be forged into pruning-hooks, and the scythes and swords into ploughshares, and when the lion shall lie with the lamb."[350]

For us there is a Eucharistic theme in these Biblical prophecies.

Plowshares till the earth so the wheat that will become our bread can grow.
Pruning hooks tend to grape vines which will become our wine. God calls
us to transform weapons into tools that enhance life, tools with which we
can, as the Psalmist writes, "satisfy the desires of every living creature."

The Christian hope is that shalom one day will extend across the
world, in all relations. Every meal is an opportunity to start living shalom.
Choosing not to eat meat is the single most important effort a person can
make on behalf of animals. It's a genuinely positive choice. By eating a
vegetarian diet, you take part in ending the exploitation of animals.
Sometimes people express their pity with vegetarians. "You must miss
meat," someone says, pointing with her fork to a fillet. But there is no reason to pity a vegetarian. One can be proud of choosing a compassionate
lifestyle.

Liturgy after the Liturgy

Within the Orthodox tradition, people speak of "the Liturgy after the
Liturgy." This is a reminder that worship doesn't end when the formal
church service ends, but continues on in all aspects of our daily lives.
"'Let us go forth in peace' is the last commandment of the Liturgy,"
writes Bishop Kallistos of Diokleia. "What does it mean? It means, surely, that the conclusion of the Divine Liturgy is not an end but a beginning.
Those words, 'Let us go forth in peace,' are not merely a comforting epi-
logue. They are a call to serve and bear witness." Since the Eucharist is
offered "in all things, and for all things," Kallistos explains, it "involves
service not just for all persons, but ministry to the whole creation, to all
created things."[351]
The "Liturgy after the Liturgy" has been described as making a connection between the Lord's Table and the common table. The breaking of
the bread of Eucharist should shine through in all the meals of the week,
turning them into a celebration of the joy and peace that God wishes for
all creatures.

ABBOT CIARAN AND BROTHER FOX:
A COMPASSIONATE CHURCH

PELLE REMEMBERS: *Finally we got the laboratory door open and rushed up the winding staircase to the second floor. Peter went first and I ran after and filmed. I was so excited that I held the video camera upside-down.*

We found her in a little room. She was quiet – didn't make a sound.

Off we went. Peter's back. The rustling of his jacket. The squeaking of our shoes. His short, intensive steps in the corridor and then carefully down the staircase – still no police!

Puppy in his arms, he ran out of the building and disappeared under the trees as he made his way toward the lot where the rental car was parked.

Helena stood on the roof of the building's entrance, a smile spreading across her face. The sun rose. It was April, the World Day for Laboratory Animals. *A few minutes later, the first police car arrived. Helena and I welcomed them.*

In jail: When I returned to the cell after my morning walk around the track, the mail had come. I lay outstretched on the orange blanket and read Helena's letter. "Just got in new towels. A small event. A priest was just here. He didn't seem to understand the greatness of Tina's liberation. We were interrupted. Time for exercise…. You wrote that you talked to the priest. Could it be the same person? Doesn't feel like I want to have him in here again. He asked "parently" questions about what my daddy thought, and so on. His questions suggested that I wasn't behaving as I should. Although he was probably well-meaning in his way. Nothing that I want to be repeated, however…. The one who makes the food seems to have lost all fantasy and inspiration. Peas today again + bread."

Social Love

The saints exemplify the power of love in action. They show us that individuals can take many steps to defend animals. One person can change the world for the better by deciding not to eat meat, boycotting products that are tested on animals, volunteering at the animal shelter, and influencing family and friends by his or her positive example. People have the greatest power, however, when they act communally. We need movements that apply the Christian message of love on a broad level. This is what John Paul II (1920–2005) called "social love."[352] Let's look at some examples.

The Bible Christian Church – a movement that originated in England and later found its way to Philadelphia – has been credited with launching the vegetarian movement in the West. The English Vegetarian Society, founded in 1847, grew out of this church.

Vegetarianism and pacifism were hallmarks of a Russian Christian movement called the Dukhobors, or "spirit-wrestlers." They suffered harsh persecution by the Tsar, and many of them immigrated to Canada at the end of the nineteenth century.[353] The Dukhobors were supported by Leo Tolstoy, who inspired many similar non-violent movements. The last pacifist organization to be closed by the new Bolshevik authorities in 1929 was the Tolstoyan Vegetarian Society in Moscow.[354]

By the end of the 1800s, anti-vivisection activists in England had organized into a strong movement, in which Christians played an important role. The Royal Society for the Prevention of Cruelty to Animals, founded by Anglican priest Arthur Broome in 1824, was based on "the Christian Faith and on Christian Principles."[355] The Church Anti-Vivisection League proclaimed that "The torture of God's sentient creatures is a sin."[356]

While some organizations have lobbied for better treatment of animals, others have taken a more direct approach. "Bull-baiting," a once popular form of entertainment in England, involves tormenting a cornered bull by repeatedly setting dogs on the animal. In 1805, a group of Quakers from Brighton, England organized to surround a baited bull to protect him from attack.[357]

New organizations working for animals have formed over the last few decades. The German organization *Aktion Kirche und Tiere* (Action for Church and Animals) works on the principle that "our older brothers and sisters in creation should have a place in our churches, that they should be respected and protected from human exploitation." [358] The Christian Vegetarian Association (CVA) describes itself as "an international, non-denominational ministry of believers dedicated to respectfully promoting healthy, Christ-centered and God-honoring living among Christians." CVA volunteers staff tables and hand out brochures at events, on Christian campuses, and outside of churches. One volunteer reports on passing out brochures at a Christian rock festival in Mississippi: "Everyone was VERY receptive. I heard teenagers who glanced at the brochure, tell their parents: 'See, I told you we shouldn't eat animals.'" [359]

Christian activists have also used films as a way to spread their message. In our local church we hosted a viewing and discussion of *The Peaceable Kingdom*, a documentary about the Farm Sanctuary movement in the United States.

The CVA and *Aktion Kirche und Tiere* represent only a small number of Christians. Can concern for animals grow into a broad Christian movement? We are hopeful that it can. In forming a new attitude toward animals, there is a lot to draw on from the Christian worldview that self-giving love should be a pattern for how we lead our lives; that service is better than egoistic exercises of power; and that God prefers mercy to sacrifice. Christians can never shrug off the challenge of the vegetarian movement. Love might require us to change our lifestyle, or even suffer discomfort for the sake of others. But we cannot reject love, for, as Scripture informs us, "those who abide in love abide in God, and God abides in them." [360]

An Unusual Monastery

After years of studies in Rome, Ciaran of Saighir returned to his home country of Ireland to work as a missionary. According to legend, the sixth century saint settled into a simple hermitage in the woods. One day he encountered a boar hiding in the shadow of a tree. The animal had never seen a human before, and fled in fright. Over time, Ciaran won the boar's trust. The animal came to live with Ciaran, building himself a little "cell." More animals joined them: a fox, a badger, a wolf, and a deer. They lived together as monks under their abbot Ciaran.

Brother Fox was tempted to abandon the vegetarian diet of the monastery. One day he stole Ciaran's shoes and carried them off to his old dwelling in the forest, intending to eat the leather. When Ciaran realized what he had done, he sent Brother Badger to fetch him. Brother Badger found Brother Fox ready to gnaw his master's slippers, and dragged the disobedient monk back to the monastery. "Why, brother, did you do this ill deed, which it becomes not monks to do?" Ciaran asked Brother Fox. "Look, our water is sweet and free to us, and food is here for us all alike to share. And if you had a longing, as is your nature, to eat flesh, Almighty God would have made it for you from the roots of these trees, if we had asked Him."[361]

This legend is an illustration of what it means to be a Christian community. The unusual monastery is a miniature image of a gentle church. The relationships are not free from friction, but they find ways of living together. It is an animal-conscious church that reflects on its eating habits, a church that takes the Biblical prophecies about a world in peace seriously. They don't merely preach on these texts, they live them.

Convincing wolves and deer to live in harmony together is best left to legends. Our ambitions have to be more modest. Learning more about the animals' situation in light of the Christian faith can be a first step. We as a Christian community must also be open to the voice of God speaking to us today. Quaker theologian and peace advocate Emilia Fogelklou (1878–1972) writes, "in every given moment wait on the stream of life that flows from the one who said: 'See, I am making all things new.'"[362]

The Calling of the Church

The church is not a building, not employees, not hymns and organ music. It might contain all of these things, but they are not the heart of it. "The true church," writes Catholic theologian Werner Jeanrond, "is indeed everywhere where people genuinely attempt to respond to God's call and help to build God's world."[363]

Jesus went to the synagogue on the Sabbath, and there met a man with a crippled hand. His opponents watched him carefully, "to see whether he would heal the fellow on the sabbath day, so that they could denounce him." Jesus called the man to his side and then asked the crowd: "On the sabbath day is it permitted to do good or do evil, to save life or to destroy it?"[364]

In the book of Leviticus, God instructs the people: "Be holy because I, the LORD your God, am holy." Many of Jesus' contemporaries saw themselves as members of a people 'set apart.' Their strict observance of the laws of Moses – including keeping the Sabbath – was a way for them to distinguish themselves from pagans and sinners. But Jesus surprised and angered many of them by insisting on other priorities. "Jesus' understanding of God as compassionate and of the norm for Israel's development as compassion," writes New Testament scholar Marcus Borg, "accounted for his opposition to the quest for holiness"[365] Rather than "Be holy because your Father is holy," Jesus preached "Be compassionate just as your Father is compassionate."[366] God has compassion for all – "makes the sun rise on the evil and the good, and sends rain on the just and the unjust" – and so Israel should have compassion for all, including sinners, outcasts and enemies.[367]

Jesus' inclusive compassion is a model for the church, and should be raised up as a core value. As God's compassion extends to all suffering individuals – human and non-human alike –, so should the church embrace all people and all beings. Every collective act of compassion strengthens our identity as a Christian church.

Revival

"I have been viewing myself as a 'spirit-filled' Christian since my conversion in 1987," writes a woman from the United States, "and have attended several types of congregations, including Pentecostal, but am not currently attending a church now. The only time in 18 years of sermons, Bible studies, prayer meetings, fellowships, lectures, and Christian radio shows that I have heard animal rights or vegetarianism mentioned was a WARNING by a pastor that these things were related to the New Age movement and therefore ungodly."[368] One Pentecostal church journal pronounces that the "doctrinaire and unnatural decision to become vegetarian, or to put the rights of animals above those of man, is sinful and cannot be reconciled to a Christian life."[369] Shouldn't "spirit-filled" Christians be the first to embrace all of God's works? After all, God's spirit and power flows through all of creation — humans and animals alike. Psalm 104 proclaims:

> *How many are your works, O LORD!*
> *In wisdom you made them all;*
> *the earth is full of your creatures. . .*
> *When you hide your face,*
> *they are terrified;*
> *when you take away their breath,*
> *they die and return to the dust.*
> *When you send your Spirit,*
> *they are created,*
> *and you renew the face of the earth.*[370]

This indwelling nature of the spirit is well expressed when the author of the book of Wisdom turns to God and says, "you spare all, since all is yours, Lord, lover of life! For your imperishable spirit is in everything!"[371]

The power of the spirit is illustrated in a passage in Per Olov Enquist's novel *Lewi's Journey*. In the mid-1890s, a Pentecostal revival swept across Wales. Even deep in the coal mines, men were touched by the spirit. "That was when they caught sight of the dumb beasts," explained Efraim, one of the books' protagonists. "The mine horses, which had previously been whipped and abused down there in the mine passageways — yes, let me tell you, those poor miserable nags never saw the light of day, they endured blows and lashes and oaths and were subjected to abuse—those mine horses started acting confused when their former persecutors gave voice to prayers and practically snuggled up to the poor horses. They were used to curses and the whip! When all that stopped they couldn't recognize their masters. Now the men started each shift with communal prayers and Bible reading, and the horses were transformed. They grew very nervous, began to neigh and whinny, as if they were giving voice to prayers and asking if their tormentors had been whisked away to eternal punishment. God's spirit had reached even those poor horses. They would stand there whinnying with amazement and inexpressible joy, as if they were praising the Savior; that was the animals speaking in tongues."[372]

This story reminds us of the surprising, transformative power of the Holy Spirit. Those touched by the holy will see their fellow creatures in a new light. This is an inspiring vision for all Christian churches.

$$- 20 -$$

ANIMALS AS JUDGES

ON THE THURSDAY BEFORE EASTER, Leo Tolstoy took a lift home from some men who were going to fetch wood from a forest outside of Moscow. Passing through a village, they witnessed a group of men dragging a pig to slaughter. "It squealed in a dreadful voice," wrote Tolstoy afterwards, "resembling the shrieking of a man." One of the butchers ran a knife into the pig's throat. The pig screamed even louder, broke free and ran away, covered in blood. Soon the men cornered the animal and knocked him to the ground. They continued to cut his throat.

When at last the pig was silent, the cart-driver sighed heavily. "Do men really not have to answer for such things?"[373]

In an earlier chapter, we mentioned Jesus' teaching on the final judgment and asked whether or not animals belong to "the least of these." Now we want to reflect further on this theme. Is God's judgment relevant to us, here and now?

According to traditional Christian theology, God holds everyone accountable for the choices they make in their lives. People have different ideas about when this trial takes place: directly after death, perhaps, or at the end of time. While we tend to think of the judgment as condemnation and punishment, contemporary academic theologians often speak of it as an eye-opening encounter with the truth. If this is correct, then we should open our lives to judgment now; truth is too important to be postponed. Werner Jeanrond describes judgment as a "disarming, liberating and creative" encounter with God; the starting point for a new way of living that leads to authentic relations.[374] If this is the case, we should welcome God's judgment over our lives. It can help us evaluate all of our relationships: with ourselves, with others, and with God. Are they true, righteous, and loving?

Many moral tales about human relationships to animals contain a judgment theme. Looking at them can help shed light on our dealings with fellow creatures.

Earlier we shared part of a story from the Egyptian church about Jesus' encounter with an abused donkey. At the end of the story, Jesus exercises his judgment. "Woe to you, that you do not hear how it complains to the Creator in heaven and cries out for mercy," he warns. "But threefold woes to him about whom it cries out and complains in its pain." Jesus heals the animal's wounds. Then he says to the donkey's owner: "from now on do not beat it any more, so that you too may find mercy."[375] These parting words were echoed by Rabbi Gamliel III in the second century, "Whosoever has compassion upon his fellow creatures, upon him will God have compassion."[376] The Jewish text II Enoch, possibly written in the time of Jesus, suggests that the souls of animals will be kept alive to the great judgment, where "they will accuse man, if he feed them ill."[377]

The idea that animals can testify in the heavenly courtroom recurs in a story about the esteemed Muslim Abu Darda. Shortly before his death, he said to his four-legged companion: "Oh my camel, don't argue with me before our Lord and Sustainer. I never let you work more than you were capable of."[378]

Our religious traditions teach us that "the greatest" experience in a person's existence – one's judgment before God – is inseparably tied to one's relation to "the smallest" – the most defenseless creatures of the earth. Jesus embraced this theology of reversal: the last in the world's order is the *first* in God's. Whatever is done for "the least" is done also for the greatest – the King, the Christ. Many writers have addressed our treatment of animals in relationship to divine judgment, including the English poet William Blake (1757-1827), the Swedish author Axel Munthe (1857-1949), and the Nobel prize winners Selma Lagerlöf (1858-1940) and J.M. Coetzee (1940-). "Kill not the moth nor butterfly," Blake warned, "for the Last Judgement draweth nigh."[379]

We haven't encountered this idea in modern works of systematic theology, nor heard it preached in church. But it appears in some important medieval texts.

"It is God's custom to care for all his creatures, both the greatest and the least," reads *De divinis moribus* (The Ways of God), probably written by a Dutch or Flemish Dominican in the late thirteenth century. "We should likewise care for creatures, whatsoever they are, in the sense that we use them in conformity with the divine purpose, in order that they may not bear witness against us in the day of judgement."[380]

According to *Dives and Pauper* (the Rich Man and the Poor Man), an English moral treatise written at the beginning of the 15th century, it is permitted to slaughter animals for food and clothing. But humans sin "full grievously" if they torment animals or birds beyond what is necessary for survival. "For God that make all hath care of all, and He will take vengeance upon all that misuse His creatures."[381] The threat of divine retribution is mentioned twice and is tied to the Bible text that states that God will "arm creation to punish his enemies."[382] The animal abuser is portrayed as an enemy of God. Grievous sin, vengeance, enmity – the author uses the strongest possible religious expressions to condemn cruelty. This strong language is necessary because we often don't see violence against animals for what it is.

Some Christians argue that human exploitation of animals is God's will. One American preacher attacks animal rights activists who "would strip beef cattle of their holy purpose as nourishment for both people and land as they organize them into useless, worthless beings 'put out to pasture' for no reason. How terrible to exist for no reason, to have no place in the scheme of things!"[383] That animals could exist for their own purpose seems implausible to him. Eugen Drewermann, a psychotherapist and one of Germany's most well know theologians, recounts a similar argument made by a "today famous German bishop." He told Drewermann's theology class that the best thing that can happen to fish and hares is to be eaten by humans, since it fulfills their place in the order of creation. The students answered with approving laughter. This "appetizing theology" relieved them from feeling guilty about killing animals for food.[384]

People have always found reasons to exploit animals. The harsh condemnation of animal abuse found in the story of Jesus and the donkey and in *Dives and Pauper* serves to pierce through those protective layers of excuses.

Conformity

We tend to adapt our personal values and behavior to our social context. If most people think that slavery is acceptable, there is a good chance that we will share that point of view. Conformity is a problem when it supports ingrained forms of oppression.

Prejudices about animals run deep in our society, making them difficult to uncover. Even good and otherwise clear-sighted people often contribute to the oppression of animals. Their example provides further justification for meat-eating. It's difficult to do right when many people are doing wrong. It's even more difficult when your own role models are doing wrong. But the judgment falls on each of us as individuals. We can't excuse our own lies and violence by pointing to what someone else did. This is also a principle in international law. The war crimes trials that followed World War II established the right and duty of all people to disobey immoral laws in their home countries. Germans who ran death camps were convicted of criminal acts even though they argued that they were "just following orders."

Sometimes it's appropriate to try to stop cruelty using nonviolent civil disobedience. But we don't need to break the law in order to live with care for animals. We do, however, need to break with the opinions and lifestyles of the majority of people.

At Heaven's Door

The Swedish author Axel Munthe (1857-1949) was trained as a physician. He lived and worked in cities throughout Europe before retiring to the

Italian island of Capri. In his youth he had been a passionate hunter, but with time he concluded that the only good reason to join a hunting party was to protect the animals. He once disrupted a grouse hunt by chasing the birds away while his friends were sleeping. "After that," he wrote, "I was never again invited to join a hunting party in that place."[385]

Munthe's commitment to animals shines through in his best-selling book *The Story of San Michele*, a partly-autobiographical account of his latter years. The book culminates in a dream sequence – at the same time comical and spiritually rich. The narrator dies and is taken to heaven. He is looking forward to meeting Saint Francis, but instead finds himself in the Hall of Judgment before a tribunal of narrow-minded saints and prophets. His life is picked apart, detail by detail. The judges become inflamed when they find out that he brought his dog with him.

> "A dog at the gates of Heaven," roared Habakkuk, "a dog, an unclean beast!"
>
> It was too much for me.
>
> "He is not an unclean beast," I shouted back, glaring angrily at Habakkuk, "he was created by the same God who created you and me. If there is a Heaven for us, there must also be a Heaven for the animals, though you grim old prophets, so fierce and stalwart in your holiness, have forgotten all about them. So for the matter of that did you, Holy Apostles," I went on losing my head more and more. "Or why did you omit in your Holy Scriptures to record a single saying of our Lord in defense of our brethren?"
>
> "The Holy Church to which I belonged on earth has never taken any interest in the animals," interrupted St. Anastasius, "nor do we wish to hear anything about them in Heaven."[386]

The judges condemn him: "To Hell! To Hell!" In the terrible silence that followed, he feels "abandoned by God and man."

But then he thinks he hears the sound of birds. A warbler lands on his shoulder and sings:

> "You saved the life of my grandmother, my aunt and my three brothers and sisters from torture and death by the hand of man on that rocky island. Welcome! Welcome!"
>
> At the same moment a skylark picked at my finger and twittered to me:
>
> "I met a flycatcher in Lapland who told me that when you were a boy you mended the wing of one of his ancestors and warmed his frozen body near your heart, and as you opened your hand to set him free you kissed him and said: 'Godspeed little brother! Godspeed little brother!' Welcome! Welcome!"
>
> "Help me little brother! Help me little brother!"
>
> "I will try, I will try," sang the skylark as he unfolded his wings and flew away with a trill of joy, "I will trrrrrry!"

Saint Francis soon arrives, surrounded by birds. He stands at the condemned man's side and says nothing, but looks at the judges "with his wonderful eyes, those eyes that neither God nor man nor beast could meet with anger in theirs."[387] Acquitted, the narrator is able at last to rest his head on Francis' shoulder.

Standing on the side of animals can have deeper implications than we may realize in the moment. To mend the wing of a bird is to step into God's reign. There we never dwell alone. The saints are by our side.

— Epilogue —
THE SPIRITUALITY OF EVERYDAY LIFE

ACCORDING TO LEGEND, an angel once offered the Irish hermit Kevin of Glendalough (d. 618) to level four mountains to the ground in order to there build a monastery. But Kevin declined, saying: "I have no wish that the creatures of God should be moved because of me."[388]

Kevin's fellow Irishman, Molua mac Ocha (d. 609), is best known for founding many monasteries, but also lived as a hermit. At his death, a legend tells, a fellow abbot came upon a weeping bird on the side of a path. An angel appeared to the abbot and explained to him that all of the animals were in mourning because the saint "never killed any creature, little or big."[389] Within Celtic Christianity – the church that thrived in the British Isles in the first millennium after Jesus – it was considered a sign of holiness to never have injured a bird.[390]

Like Kevin and Molua before him, the Trappist monk Thomas Merton – one of the most celebrated Christian authors from the United States – belongs in the tradition of the compassionate hermit. One November morning in 1965, Merton was saying his morning prayers under the pine trees in front of his Kentucky hermitage. "I saw a wounded deer limping along in the field, one leg incapacitated," he wrote afterwards. "I was terribly sad at this and began weeping bitterly. Then something quite extraordinary happened. I will never forget standing there weeping and looking at the deer standing still looking at me questioningly for a long time, a minute or so. The deer bounded off without any sign of trouble."[391]

When we see the world through eyes of compassion, we take part in the healing ministry of Christ, as the stories of Kevin, Molua and Merton testify. Compassionate people don't wish to harm or take the life of another. They strive to promote human and animals life. It isn't about making ourselves worthy before God through a flurry of righteous deeds.

It isn't about producing compassion; compassion is already within us, stamped in our hearts. We need to say Yes to it, give it room to grow, apply it to new areas.

Throughout church history, people have sought spiritual advice from hermits. Hermits have lived at the margins, allowing them to view the rest of society from a different perspective. Their insights can help the rest of us live our day-to-day lives with more integrity.

"Today—carnavale—farewell to the flesh, wrote Thomas Merton in 1953 – many years before the emergence of the modern animal rights movement. "It is a poor joke to be merry about leaving the flesh, as if we were to return to it once again. What would be the good of Lent if it were only temporary?"[392] Merton was an early critic of the new methods of large-scale, intensive agriculture that came into existence after the World War II – hailed by many as modern, efficient and economical means of producing food. In 1966 he wrote: "factory farming exerts a violent and unnatural force upon the living organisms of animals and birds."[393] In the years since, factory farms have grown in both number and scale, all but wiping out family farms in industrialized nations. Never before have human beings inflicted so much suffering on so many of God's creatures.

The situation in the world makes the spirituality of compassion urgent. For the person who is drawn to this lifestyle, the door is open. You don't have to join any particular organization or belong to any particular denomination. You don't need to build your own hermitage in the woods in order to accompany Kevin, Molua and Merton on their walk with Christ. The way of compassion that they have chosen leads straight into the ordinary, earthly life: relations, get-togethers, meals. Everyday life is the home of compassion. There you can choose to step into this great spiritual tradition.

— Further Reading —

HERE IS A SAMPLING OF BOOKS on Christian animal care written in English. It's not a complete list, but enough to get you started.

Andrew Linzey, Anglican priest and Oxford scholar, has made crucial contributions to modern animal rights theology. *Animal Gospel: Christian Faith As Though Animals Mattered* (1998), a collection of short and personal essays, "speaks of my frustration, my pain, my sadness, but most of all my inner conviction that Christ-like discipleship is singularly tested in compassion to the Christ-like suffering of the weakest of all." *Christianity and the Rights of Animals* (1987) and *Animal Theology* (1994) have a more academic character but are still easy to read. *Animal Rites: Liturgies of Animal Care* (1999) is a collection of services, prayers and devotional readings for and about animals, including animal burial rites. Linzey and the Jewish theologian Dan Cohn-Sherbok are the co-authors of *After Noah: Animals and the Liberation of Theology* (1997). In *Creatures of the Same God* (2007), Linzey's discussions include "Religion and Sensitivity to Animal Suffering", "Theology as if Animals Mattered", and "Animals and Vegetarianism in Early Chinese Christianity".

Stephen Webb, associate professor of religion and philosophy at Wabash College, provides a "Biblical alternative" to the animal rights movement in his book *Good Eating* (2001). This is a thorough work that draws on the Bible, writings of the early church fathers, and modern theology. Webb writes that "there is a good case to be made that vegetarianism is a valid and valuable way of anticipating the kingdom of God by practicing what God most intends for the world." The chapter "Why Jesus Was (Probably) Not a (Strict) Vegetarian" is an interesting exploration of the controversy over Jesus' diet. He is also the author of *On God and Dogs: A Christian Theology of Compassion for Animals* (1998), a more demanding academic work.

New Testament scholar Richard Alan Young is the author of *Is God A*

Vegetarian? Christianity, Vegetarianism, and Animal Rights (1999). "The choice," he writes, "is between a meat-eating diet that celebrates a fallen world or a vegetarian diet that celebrates new life through the risen Christ." The foreword is written by Carol J. Adams, a proponent of the feminist ethics of care. She is author of the useful *The Inner Art of Vegetarianism: Spiritual Practices for Body and Soul* (2000), which includes a textbook, workbook and daily meditations. "Vegetarianism is not so much a diet as an acknowledgement of relationships," she writes, "between your choice of food and your body's health; between yourself and your sisters and brothers, the animals; and between your actions and the earth's health." Adams is also author of *Prayers for Animals* (2004). www.caroljadams.com

J.R. Hyland (1933-2007) was an ordained evangelical minister. She wrote *God's Covenant with Animals: A Biblical Basis for the Humane Treatment of All Creatures* (2000), a thorough review of animal themes within the Bible, including the Old Testament prophets' critique of animal sacrifice. "The prophets taught that God's blessings would abound only in a world where human beings rejected violence and 'no longer taught war,'" she writes. "But the journey toward that peaceable kingdom demanded that the sacrifice of animals stop."

The Dominion of Love: Animal Rights According to the Bible (2002), by Norm Phelps, is a powerful and well-written argument for vegetarianism from a Biblical perspective. It includes commentary on a wide range of Bible texts that might come up in discussions with meat-eaters.

Good News for All Creation: Vegetarianism as Christian Stewardship (2002), by Stephen R. Kaufman and Nathan Braun (of the Christian Vegetarian Association), is an excellent introduction to faith-based vegetarianism. "The Bible is God's handbook for our lives," the book claims, making it ideal for Bible-oriented Christians. They also give good advice for how to promote Christian vegetarianism.

Matthew Scully, a former speechwriter to President George W. Bush, is the author of *Dominion: The Power of Man, the Suffering of Animals, and the Call to Mercy* (2002). "How we treat our fellow creatures is only one more way in which each one of us, every day, writes our own epigraph," he writes, "bearing into the world a message of light and life or just more darkness and death, adding to the world's joy or to its despair." Beautifully written, often witty. www.matthewscully.com

The Lost Religion of Jesus: Simple Living and Nonviolence in Early Christianity (2000), by Keith Akers, argues that Jesus didn't want to start a new religion, but rather a reform movement based in simple living and nonviolence. The reader might not be convinced of his thesis that Jesus was a vegetarian, but Akers presents many bold, refreshing theories about the early Church. Written in excellent prose. www.compassionatespirit.com

Gary Kowalski is a Unitarian Universalist pastor and author of *The Bible According to Noah: Theology as if Animals Mattered* (2001). Using Old Testament stories as his starting point, Kowalski develops a theology of reverence for all living creatures. "My hope is that, when rightly understood and freshly interpreted, the Bible can awaken us to a new sense of appreciation for the gift (and the responsibility) that has been placed into our care." His earlier book, *The Souls of Animals* (1999) takes a look at the spiritual and emotional lives of animals.

Mary Lou Randour, a professional psychologist, ties together spiritual insights from various faith traditions and animal advocacy in her readable book, *Animal Grace: Entering a Spiritual Relationship with Our Fellow Creatures* (2002).

The biologist Charles Birch and the theologian Lukas Vischer are co-authors of *Living with the Animals: The Community of God's Creatures* (1997).

Judy Carman's *Peace to All Beings* (2003) is a prayer book for spiritually-oriented animal rights activists, drawing on various religious traditions.

In *Animals and Man: A State of Blessedness* (1992), author Joanne Stefanatos shares stories of many saints from the Eastern Christian tradition. Stefanatos is a veterinarian and animal rights advocate.

They Shall Not Hurt or Destroy: Animal Rights & Vegetarianism in the Western Religious Traditions (1995), by Vasu Murti, is available for purchase through the Christian Vegetarian Association at www.christian-veg.org/materials.htm

The Jesuit priest and peace activist John Dear ties vegetarianism to nonviolence in *Christianity and Vegetarianism: Pursuing the Nonviolence of Jesus* www.jesusveg.com/christveg.pdf.

Two valuable scholarly articles are "The Status of Animals in Biblical and Christian Thought: A Study in Colliding Values" by Rod Preece and David Fraser (2000), available on www.psyeta.org/sa/sa8.3/fraser.shtml (July 7, 2005); and "Christianity" by Robin Attfield, in *A Companion to Environmental Philosophy* (2001), Jamieson, Dale, ed.

Anthologies

Animals and Christianity: A Book of Readings (1988), edited by Andrew Linzey and Tom Regan, compiles relevant essays from church history, including John Wesley's *The General Deliverance* (on animals' afterlife), Leo Tolstoy's *The First Step* (on vegetarianism) and John Calvin's *The Tyranny of Vegetarianism.*

In the scholarly *Animals on the Agenda* (1998), edited by Andrew Linzey and Dorothy Yamamoto, twenty contemporary theologians discuss the status of animals in theology, ethics and society.

Helen Waddell (1889-1965) is the editor of *Beasts and Saints* (1934), a collection of stories about interactions between animals and the Desert Fathers and Celtic Saints. A treasure, but hard to come by.

Awe for the Tiger, Love for the Lamb: A Chronicle of Sensibility to Animals (2002), edited by Rod Preece, is a must-have reference book for anyone who is interested in the history of animal care.

Internet

There are, of course, many relevant websites for Christian animal advocates. Rather than providing a long list here, we refer you to the "Christian Vegetarian Links" page at www.christianveg.org

— NOTES —

[1]Merton (2001), p. 91. We were alerted to this and several other Merton quotes, through Einarsson (2005).

[2]A philosopher asked St Anthony of Egypt (251–356): "Father, how can you be so happy when you are deprived of the consolation of books?" Anthony replied "My book, O philosopher, is the nature of created things, and any time I want to read the words of God, the book is before me." From *The Wisdom of the Desert* (p. 62), edited by Thomas Merton, quoted on www.onegodsite.net/nature (February 7, 2006). Merton himself often expressed this creation-oriented theology. He wrote after watching deer one evening: "It is an awe-inspiring thing–the Mantu or 'spirit' shown in the running of the deer, the 'deerness' that sums up everything and is sacred and marvelous." Merton (2003), p. 125. "This is the reality I need, the vestige of God in His creatures." (p. 45).

Meister Eckhart (1260–1327) wrote: "The Father speaks the Son from his entire power and he speaks him in all things. All creatures are words of God." Eckhart & Fox (1991), p. 58. The same passage in a different translation: "The Father speaks the Son out of all his power, and he speaks in him all things. All created things are God's speech." Eckhart (1981), p. 205. "[…] each creature is full of God and is a book [about God]." Eckhart & Fox (1991), p. 79. "All creatures talk ... about 'God'." Eckhart (1961), p. 94.

The German-Polish poet and Christian mystic Angelus Silesius (1624–77) wrote: "The creatures are the voice of the eternal Word." Quoted in Bastaire (1996), p. 78.

[3]Woolman (1909[orig.1774]), pp. 320–321.

[4]Phelps (2002a) [an unpaginated electronic work].

[5]*The New Interpreter's Bible* (1994), p. 346.

[6]Mark 16:15 (NIV).

[7]Wisdom 11:24 (New Jerusalem Bible).

[8]"St. Cuthbert's Birds and Bartholomew, the Hermit of Farne" in Waddell, ed. (1995), pp. 94–95.

[9]Luke 22:26 (NIV), see also Mark 10:42–44 (NIV).

[10]John 13:13–15 (NIV).

[11]Schottroff (1992), p. 57. In this we follow the analysis of contemporary feminist theologians and biblical scholars, who argue that Jesus presented a radical critique of social inequality, including gender inequality. See, for example, Elisabeth Schüssler Fiorenza's *In Memory of Her*. These views are not universally held, however. Kathleen Corley concludes her book *Women & the Historical Jesus: Feminist Myths of Christian Origins:* "Jesus' teaching clearly involved critique of rank and class, but it included no recognition of sexism in his culture." Corley (2002), p. 145.

[12]Philippians 2:6–7.

[13]We write "feel" because it is not obvious that meat is in the interest of meat eaters. The high consumption of animal-based food among Westerners is not ideal from a human health perspective.

[14]"St. Jerome and the Lion and the Donkey," in Waddell, ed. (1995), p. 35.

[15]Quoted in Sorrell (1988), p. 74.

[16]We have used Richard Sharpe's translation of Adomnán of Iona (1995[orig.690]), p. 150. With one exception: rather than referring to the heron as "it," we've followed Helen Waddell's translation, referring to the bird as "she." See "St. Columba and the Crane" in Waddell, ed. (1995), pp. 44–45.

Note that Sharp translates the Latin *grus* with "heron" rather than "crane." He explains why in note 203, p. 311.

[17]Young (1999), p. 54.

[18]Genesis 1:29 (NIV).

[19]Young (1999), p. 20. Young discusses what kind of food the biblical authors may have meant by "seed-bearing plants and every tree that has fruit with seed in it."

[20]Andrén, ed. (1994), p. 29. Andrén gives PG (Patrologiae Cursus Completus, Series Graeca) 44:284 as his source.

[21]We have benefited from Tomas Einarsson's fine treatment of the fasting tradition in Eastern Christianity. See Einarsson (2005) pp. 7, 22, 46 (on Basil the Great), & 131 (on Jerome).

[22]Malaty (1993), p. 228. This work is also published electronically. www.stgeorge-sporting.org/coptic/thefasten.htm (May 4, 2006).

[23]Webb (2001), p. 59.

[24]Genesis 2:8–9. Westermann (1984) p. 208.

[25]Genesis 1:26–28 (NIV).

[26]Psalm 72:12–14 (NIV).

[27]Wenham (1987), p. 33. See also *Brueggemann* (1982), p. 32; *New Interpreter's Bible* (1994) p. 346; Jónsson (1988), p. 220.

[28]Quoted in Preece & Fraser (2000).

[29]Quoted in Thomas (1984), p. 155.

[30]Genesis 1:31 (NIV).

[31]Genesis 9:3–4 (NIV).

[32]Genesis 9:4. Cassuto (1964), p. 126; von Rad (1972), pp. 131–132; Cassuto (1961), pp. 58–59.

[33]1 Samuel 8:4–22 (NIV).

[34]Matthew 19:8 (NIV). The mosaic law can be found in Deuteronomy 24:1. Men could legally abandon their wives, forcing many women into economic desperation and social ostracism. Jesus' teaching has been interpreted as a rejection of this injustice.

[35]Isaiah 11:6–9 (NIV).

[36]Bauckham (1998b), p. 59.

[37]Mark 12–13 reads: "and the Spirit immediately drove him out into the wilderness. He was in the wilderness forty days, tempted by Satan; and he was with the wild beasts; and the angels waited on him." We have read three interpretations of this passage: 1. The animals emphasize that Jesus was alone, without human company; 2. The wild animals are a part of Satan's attack on Jesus; and 3. Jesus lives in peace and harmony with the wild animals. The latter "is the interpretation which has been argued most fully and persuasively in recent discussion, and probably now commands the support of a majority of exegetes," writes Bauckham. "Mark represents Jesus as the eschatological Adam who, having resisted Satan, instead of succumbing to temptation as Adam did, then restores paradise: he is at peace with the animals and the angels serve him." Bauckham (1994), pp. 6–7.

[38]Power Bratton (1988), p. 36.

[39]Quoted in Preece, ed. (2002), p. 89. A Swedish translation of the Latin original is found in Birgitta (1958), p. 293.

[40]Luke 10:27–37 (NIV). The Levites tended to practical and religious tasks in the Temple, but were subservient to the priests, who performed sacrificial rituals.

[41]Hammar (2000), p. 110.

[42]Libell (2001), p.322.

[43]Libell (2001), p. 325.

[44]http://nobelprize.org/peace/laureates/1952/schweitzer-lecture-e.html (May 4, 2005).

[45]Matthew 15:24. See also Mark 7:24–29.

[46]Hammar (2000), p. 49.

[47]Dostoevsky (1991[orig.1879]), p. 319.

[48]Randour (2000), pp. 6–7.

[49]One of his early biographers wrote of Francis of Asissi: "Following the footprints imprinted on creatures, he follows his Beloved everywhere." The Remembrance of the Desire of a Soul by Thomas of Celano, in Armstrong; Hellmann; & Short, eds. (2000), p. 353.

[50]Gaffney (1998), p. 108.

[51]"Of Charity Towards Beasts," in Jammes (2004[orig.1903]) [an unpaginated electronic work].

[52]Quoted in Claesson (2000), p. 147.

[53]Compare with Thomas Merton's insight that all beings "are all part of one another and all involved in one another." Merton, "Marxism and Monastic Perspectives" (1970), quoted in Fox (2000), p. 277.

[54]"Of Charity Towards Beasts," in Jammes (2004[orig.1903]) [an unpaginated electronic work].

[55]See I and Thou, by Martin Buber (1878–1965).

[56]Woolman (1909[orig.1774]), pp. 181–182. Compare with 1 John 4:20 (NIV): "If anyone says, 'I love God,' yet hates his brother, he is a liar. For anyone who does not love his brother, whom he has seen, cannot love God, whom he has not seen."

[57]Merton (2003), p. 112.

[58]"A not-so-shaggy dog story, complete with happy ending," www.msnbc.msn.com/ id/6778468 (January 24, 2006).

[59]Mason (2005), p. 91.

[60]Kowalski (1999), pp. 18–19.

[61]Job 12:7 (NIV).

[62]See e.g. Preece, ed. (2002), pp. 89–90.

[63]From a Coptic collection of sayings and stories known as "bustan al-rohbaan" (The Monks' Garden). www.coptic.net/articles/ParadiseOfDesertFathers.txt (April 5, 2006).

[64]"Article XXI: Of the Worship of the Saints" in The Augsburg Confession (1530), www.ctsfw.edu/etext/boc/ac/ (January 10, 2006).

[65]Nationalencyklopedin [Swedish National Encyclopedia] (2000).

[66]Chapter 40 of The Little Flowers of Saint Francis, p. 632 in Armstrong; Hellmann; & Short, eds. (2001).

[67]Chapter 8 of The Major Legend of Saint Francis, by Bonaventure of Bagnoregio, in Armstrong; Hellmann; & Short, eds. (2000), p. 590.

[68]Quoted in Attwater (1960), pp. 59–60. Attwater offers no reference for this quote, but it is consistent with another recorded saying of Chrysostom: "The souls of the Saints are very gentle and, loving unto man, both in regard to their own, and to strangers. And even to the unreasoning creatures they extend their gentleness. Wherefore also a certain wise man said, 'The righteous pitieth

the souls of his cattle.'" [See Proverbs 12:10 (NIV): "A righteous man cares for the needs of his animal, but the kindest acts of the wicked are cruel."]. Chrysostom, "Homilies on the Epistle to the Romans" www.newadvent.org/fathers/210229.htm (May 11, 2005).

[69]Hildegaard of Bingen (1996), p. 108.

[70]The German theologian Dietrich Bonhoeffer (1906–45) addresses the common origin of humans and animals in his analysis of the book of Genesis: "According to the Bible human beings and animals have the same kind of body! Perhaps the human being would find a helper who is a suitable partner amond these brothers and sisters – for that is what they are, the animals who have the same origin as humankind does." Bonhoeffer (1997), p. 96.

[71]See Genesis 1, 2, 3, 7 & 9. About our common destinies, see Jeremiah 7:20: "My anger and my wrath shall be poured out on this place, on human beings and animals."

[72]"Life of Melangell," in Davis & Bowie (1995), pp. 65–66. The Anglican Archbishop Rowan Williams comments that this story "dramatises the strength of contemplative resistance; it tells us that there is a place to be away from hunting." Foreword to Cluysenaar & Schwenk, eds. (2004), p. vii. Melangell's Latin name is Monacella.

[73]To name a few: Saint Neot (d. 877), monk from Glastonbury, England; Saint Petroc; the Spanish Saint Isidorus; Saint Aventine, who lived in France in the seventh century. For the last two mentioned, and other examples, see Ryder (1989), p. 34. About Petroc, see Guiley (2001), p. 254. About Neot, see Thomas (1984) p. 152; the Patron Saint Index: www.catholic-forum.com/saints/saintn45.htm; and Guiley (2001), p. 253.

[74]Eadmer (1962), pp. 89–90.

[75]Psalm 36:6 (NRSV).

[76]Matt. 10:29 (New Jerusalem). The original Greek is difficult to interpret: no sparrow falls to the ground "without your Father." Other English translations read "apart from your Father."

[77]Job 38:41 (NIV).

[78]From biographies by Reginald and Geoffrey, in Waddell, ed. (1995), pp. 73–91.

[79]More (2003[orig.1516]), p. 108.

[80]More (1992[orig.1516]), p. 42.

[81]More (1992[orig.1516]), p. 54.

[82]Turner (1992), p. 29.

[83]García-Rivera (1995) p. 2.

[84]Monahan (2002) p. 67.

[85]García-Rivera (1995). See also Mason (2005), p. 230.

[86]Clément (2002), p. 49.

[87]Adomnán of Iona (1995[orig.690]), p. 178.

[88]For more information, see "Frequently Asked Questions" on the Alternatives to Animal Testing Web Site, http://altweb.jhsph.edu (March 8, 2006); or The Johns Hopkins Center for Alternatives to Animal Testing, http://caat.jhsph.edu/.

[89]From Aquinas' *Summa Contra Gentiles*, quoted in Clarke & Linzey, eds. (1990), p. 8, 10. This is standard interpretation of Aquinas' view of animals, accepted by both critics and supporters. An alternative interpretation can be found in Deane-Drummond (2004), p. 67.

[90]From Augustine's *The Catholic and Manichaean Ways of Life*, quoted in Singer (1990), p. 129.

[91]For Stoicism's influence on Augustine's animal ethics, see Sorabji (1993) pp. 195–198. See also

Young (1999), pp. 136–137.

[92]See Harwood (1928), pp. 47–49.

[93]Bernhard (1937), p. 46.

[94]Thomas Merton addressed this issue in a note written on December 11, 1962: "I have been shocked at a notice of a new book by Rachel Carson on what is happening to birds as a result of the indiscriminate use of poisons (which do not manage to kill the insects they intend to kill). Someone will say: you worry about birds. Why not worry about people? I worry about *both* birds and people. We are in the world and part of it, and we are destoying everything because we are destroying ourselves spiritually, morally, and in every way. It is all part of the same sickness, it all hangs together." Merton (2001), p. 198.

[95]Matthew 21:31, 20:16; Luke 13:30; Mark 10:31.

[96]Luke 1:52–53.

[97]Dostoevsky (1991[orig.1879]), p. 295.

[98]Luke 9:46, 22:24; Matthew 18:1; Mark 9:34,10:37.

[99]See Mark 8:27–33: Peter is rebuked by Jesus for not accepting the way of suffering; and Eriksson, Grenholm et al. (2004), p. 71.

[100]Bauckham (1998a), p. 38.

[101]Kundera (1985), p. 277.

[102]Job 39:8–11.

[103]See Deuteronomy 15:12; Habel (1985), p. 546; and Rowley (1980), p. 248.

[104]*A Mirror of the Perfection*, chap. 12, in Armstrong; Hellmann; & Short, eds. (2001), p. 362. Compare with Matthew 5:5 (NIV): "Blessed are the meek, for they will inherit the earth."

[105]Martin Lönnebo, in *Bönboken* (2003), p. 116.

[106]Matthew 25:31–40 (NIV).

[107]Gutiérrez (1988), p. 112.

[108]From Adams' foreword in Young (1999), p. ix.

[109]Julian of Norwich (1966[orig.1373]), p. 91.

[110]Kempe (1985), p. 104.

[111]From Sitwell "Still falls the rain," quoted in Linzey & Regan, eds. (1988), p. 70.

[112]John 1:3; Ephesians 1:10; Colossians 1:20.

[113]William Bowling, quoted in Thomas (1984), p. 139.

[114]Thomas (1984), p. 140.

[115]Martin Luther (1483–1546) claimed this, e.g. in his lectures on Genesis.

[116]Proverbs 23:13–14 (NIV). See also Proverbs 22:15 and Hebrews 12:7. For examples of Christian justifications for the abuse of children, see Hill & Cheadle (1996), pp. 53–54.

[117]Quoted in Gundry-Volf (2001), p. 33. "Of all the characteristics in which the medieval age differs from the modern," writes historian Barbara Tuchman, "none is so striking as the comparative absence of interest in children." Tuchman (1979), p. 49.

[118]Mark 10:14 (NIV).

[119]Gundry-Volf (2001), p. 38.

[120]Matthew 18:1–3 (NIV).

[121]Frostin (1970), p. 25.

[122]deMause, ed. (1974), p. 7.

[123]Thomas (1984), p. 43.

[124]Quoted in Brekus (2001), p. 313.

[125]Quoted in Singer (1990), p. 203.

[126]"Catholic theology identified the image of God in man with God's spiritual powers of reason and free will," writes Marc D. Guerra in "The Affirmation of Genuine Human Dignity," http://www.acton.org/publicat/m_and_n/2001_fall/guerra.html (April 22, 2006).

[127]"Cruelty to Animals," in *The Catholic Encyclopedia, Volume IV*, www.newadvent.org (February 3, 2006).

[128]Matthew 21:14–16 (NIV).

[129]Gundry-Volf (2001), p. 46.

[130]Matthew 11:25 (NIV).

[131]*The Gospel of Pseudo-Matthew*, chap. 35, www.meta-religion.com (February 3, 2006). We were alerted to this work through Cohn-Sherbok & Linzey (1997), pp. 62–68. The keen ability of animals to perceive the divine is also highlighted in the Old Testament story of Balaam (Numbers 22:21–31). Balaam's donkey – not Balaam – recognizes God's angel.

[132]From *The Principles of Political Economy*, quoted in Wynne-Tyson, ed. (1990), p. 306.

[133]Ryder (1989), p. 174; and "Bergh, Henry," in Bekoff, ed. (1998).

[134]Lederer (1995), p. 29.

[135]www.saintjude.biz/ (June 3, 2006).

[136]Linzey (1994), chap. 2.

[137]Van de Weyer, ed. (1990), pp. 67–68.

[138]Dostoevsky (1991[orig.1879]), p. 319.

[139]"Animal Smoking Experiments," www.pcrm.org/resch/anexp/beyond/smoke_0409.html (March 8, 2006).

[140]"725 Reasons Why You Don't Want to Be an Animal in a Military Lab," www.pcrm.org/maga-zine/GM98Autumn/GM98Autumn1.html (March 8, 2006); "The Military's War on Animals," www.peta.org/feat/military (March 8, 2006); and www.animalaid.org.uk/campaign/vivi/aamsa98.htm (March 8, 2006).

[141]From Tryon's *The Complaints of the Birds and Fowls of Heaven to their Creator for the Oppressions and Violence Most Nations on the Earth do Offer Them*, quoted in Ryder (1989), p. 52.

[142]John Henry Newman (1801–90), *Parochial and Plain Sermons* (1868), quoted in Wynne-Tyson, ed. (1990), p. 339.

[143]See Psalms 104:21, 27; 147:9; 148:7–10; Isaiah 43:20; and Job 39:3.

[144]From Gregory's *Orations*, quoted in Bergmann (2005), p. 108.

[145]"Hymn to God," in Saint Gregory Nazianzen (1986), p. 7.

[146]From Tertullian's *On Prayer*, www.vatican.va/spirit/documents/spirit_20010322_tertulliano_en.html (December 20, 2005).

[147]For more information on the plight of cows in the US dairy industry, see Marcus (2005), pp. 34–37.

[148]Psalms 94:1 (NIV).

[149]Psalms 58:3, 7 (NIV). See also Psalms 18:47.

[150]*Befrielsen* (1993), p. 211.

[151]For examples of how the suffering of animals differs from that of humans, see Singer (1993), p. 60; and Rollin (1990), pp. 144–145.

[152]Psalms 157:6 (NRSV).

[153]Romans 8:26 (New Jerusalem).

[154]Romans 8:21–22 (NIV).

[155]Personal communication, April 2006.

[156]Thomas (1984), p. 139.

[157]Saramago (1994), p. 216.

[158]Beskow (1983), p. 69.

[159]Quoted in *Holy Cows*, (2005), p. 3.

[160]Linzey (2000), p. 25.

[161]Mark 10:18 (NIV).

[161]Jan Hjärpe, quoted in Palmdahl (2005), p. 88.

[162]Matthew 5:39 (NIV).

[163]The passive interpretation of Jesus' teachings is a tradition dating back to the King James translation of 1611. Wink explains: "When the court translators working in the hire of King James chose to translate *antistenai* as "*Resist* not evil," they were doing something more than rendering Greek into English. They were translating nonviolent resistance into docility. Jesus did not tell his oppressed hearers not to resist evil. [...] His entire ministry is utterly at odds with such a preposterous idea. The Greek word is made up of two parts: *anti*, a word still used in English for "against," and *histemi*, a verb that in its noun form (*stasis*) means violent rebellion, armed revolt, sharp dissension. In the Greek Old Testament, *antistenai* is used primarily for military encounters – 44 out of 71 times. It refers specifically to the moment two armies collide..." Wink (2003), pp. 10–11. Jesus' backs up his teaching on resistance, writes Wink, with three concrete examples: "if anyone strikes you on the right cheek, turn the other also; and if anyone wants to sue you and take your coat, give your cloak as well; and if any one forces you to go one mile, go also the second mile." (Matthew 5: 39–42). To the latter, Wink provides this analysis: "A soldier could impress a civilian to carry his pack one mile only; to force the civilian to go father carried with it severe penalties under military law. In this way Rome attempted to limit the anger of the occupied people and still keep its armies on the move." So going "the second mile" is a creative act of resistance to occupation. "Imagine the hilarious situation," writes Wink, "of a Roman infantryman pleading with a Jew, 'Aw, come on, please give me back my pack!' The humor of this scene may escape those who picture it through sanctimonious eyes, but it could scarcely have been lost on Jesus' hearers, who must have been regaled at the prospect of thus discomforting their oppressors." pp. 23, 25.

[164]Genesis 2:7, and 2:19. See also Phelps (2002b), p. 181.

[165]Genesis 9:8–17. See e.g. www.newadvent.org/cathen/11088a.htm, and www.word-sunday.com/Files/B/1-Lent-b/FR-1Lent-b.html (May 10, 2006).

[166]Mark 10:18 (NIV).

[167]Stendahl (2004), p. 9.

[168]Some examples: Paul's view on the relationship between faith and deeds seems to be challenged

in James 2:14; Romans and Revelation present two contrary theologies about the state; In Revelation (11:18), the enemy is portrayed as completely demonic, which contradicts the command to love the enemy – a central theme in Jesus' sermon on the mount. Hays (2001), p. 182.

[169]About the gospels' different portrayals of Jesus, see Johnson (1990), p. 6. For more details, and with a focus on ethical issues, see Hays (1996).

[170]John 8:44 (NIV). The historical background to these harsh words was the growing conflict between Christians and Jewish religious leadership. In the first letter of Paul to the Church in Thessalonica, the Jews are labeled as "the enemies of the whole human race" (2:15, New Jerusalem) – words that have been used to justify Christian anti-Semitism.

[171]Bergen (1996), p. 160. The portrayal of Jesus as anti-Jewish was not unique to Nazism – it had roots in earlier German theology. See Heschel (2001), p. 88.

[172]Julius Streicher, former editor of the Nazi newspaper *Der Stürmer*, quoted in Bieringer, Pollefeyt & Vandecasteele-Vanneuville, eds. (2001), p. 16.

[173]Svartvik (2004), p. 189.

[174]Matthew 23:23 (NIV). Some translations read "weightier," others the superlative "weightiest."

[175]Svartvik (2004), p. 190.

[176]Mark 5:13 (NIV). Compare with Matthew 8:28–34, and Luke 8:26–39.

[177]From Augustine's *The Catholic and Manichaean Ways of Life*, quoted in Singer (1990), p. 129. See also Sorabji (1993), p. 196; and Bauckham (1998a), p. 47. Critics of Jesus often refer to the episode with the swine. In a 1927 pamphlet entitled *Why I Am Not A Christian*, the prominent English philosopher Bertrand Russell wrote: "There is the instance of the Gadarene swine, where it certainly was not very kind to the pigs to put the devils into them and make them rush down the hill into the sea. You must remember that He was omnipotent, and He could have made the devils simply go away; but He chose to send them into the pigs." http://users.drew.edu/~jlenz/whynot.html (April 17, 2006).

[178]Ström (1983), p. 44.

[179]Myers et al. (1996), p. 59. Phelps (2002b), pp. 139–142.

[180]www.godeatsredmeat.com/medicine.htm (April 17, 2006).

[181]Luke 24:36–43 (NIV).

[182]Webb (2001), pp.130–132.

[183]Webb (2001), p. 131.

[184]Webb (2001), pp. 150–151. One conservative theological book explains the absence of lamb this way: "The lamb of God was Jesus himself, and he knew that he was to be crucified for the sin of the world." Drane (1979), p. 76. Compare with John 1:29 (NIV): "the Lamb of God who takes away the sin of the world!"

[185]Linzey (1994), p. 87.

[186]Young (1999), pp. 118–119. See also Webb (2001), p 128.

[187]Webb (2001), p. 135.

[188]Webb (2001), p. 228.

[189]*The Gospel of the Ebionites*, Chapter 6, in Miller, ed. (1994), p. 439.

[190]See Akers (2000). Young, Webb and Bauckham reject the idea that the Ebionites were ethical vegetarians. See Bauckham (1998b), p. 52; Webb (2001), p. 114; Young (1999), p. 97.

[191]Matthew 15:11 (NIV).

[192]Mark 7:19 (NIV).

[193]www.scripturessay.com/q425a.html (August 30, 2005).

[194]Svartvik (2004), pp. 75–91.

[195]Stendahl (2004), p. 8.

[196]"Saint Macarius of Alexandria and the Grateful Hyena," in Waddell, ed. (1995), pp. 13–15. Compare with Mark's account (8:13) of Jesus' healing of the blind man.

[197]There are many examples of the saints healing animals: Saint Malo (d. ca. 640) restored a pig to life. The legends of Saint Ciaran (d. ca. 549) and Saint Cuthbert (d. 687) tell how they each healed small birds. On Kentigern (also known as Saint Mungo), see Duckett (1959), p. 89. On Malo, see Waddell, ed. (1995), p. 53. On Ciaran, see Waddell, ed. (1995), p. 99. On Cuthbert, see Lecky (1955), p. 171. On Martin, see Monahan (2002), p. 71. On Werburga, see Waddell, ed. (1995), p. 69.

[198]The Major Legend of Saint Francis, in Armstrong; Hellmann; & Short, eds. (2000), p. 592.

[199]Bonaventure wrote that Francis "had perfectly put on Christ" (a reference to Galatians 3:27) and was "O truly the most Christian of men, who strove by perfect imitation to be conformed while living to Christ living." The Major Legend of Saint Francis, in Armstrong; Hellmann; & Short, eds. (2000), p. 531 and p. 643, respectively. For Bonaventure's ideas on "the virtue that unites all creatures in brotherhood," see Robson (1999), p. 245.

[200]From John Greenleaf Whitter's Introduction to The Journal of John Woolman, quoted on www.phillyburbs.com/undergroundrailroad/lay.shtml (April 28, 2006). On Lay, see Davis (1966), pp. 320–326.

[201]Lay (2006[orig.1737]), p. 127. See Proverbs 12:10.

[202]Thomas (1984), p. 184.

[203]On Thomas Tryon, see Thomas (1984); on Wesley (1703–91), see Preece, ed. (2002), p. 153; on Wilberforce (1759–1833), see Singer (1990), p. 221.

[204]Mabee (1970), p. 77.

[205]From a letter from Stowe to Henry Bergh (1813–1888), quoted in Wynne-Tyson, ed. (1990), p. 518.

[206]On the publisher of the Regenerator – Orson S. Murray – see Iacobbo & Iacobbo (2004), p. 63; on Alcott, see www.alcott.net, Iacobbo & Iacobbo (2004), p. 56, and on Alcott and Lane, see Watner (1982) [an unpaginated electronic work]; on Clubb, see Gregory (2001) [an unpaginated electronic work]; on Nicholson, see Hamm (1995), p. 182. Henry Ward Beecher, Frederick Douglass, and Julius Ames are also among the critics of slavery who advocated compassion for animals. On Douglass, see Spiegel (1996), pp. 107, 109; on Ames, see Scully (2002), p. 88; on Ward Beecher, see Preece, ed. (2002), p. 283. On the intersection of vegetarian and abolition movements in the US, see Iacobbo & Iacobbo (2004), pp. 62–64.

[207]Hamm (1995), p. 142.

[208]Hamm (1995), p. 182.

[209]Hamm (1995), p. 155.

[210]www.alcott.net (August 2, 2006). "Instead of using cotton, a product of slavery, Alcott designed pants suits from linen that were worn by both the males and females at Fruitlands. He baked bread for the little group and promoted the use of raw vegetarian foods to help free the women from the drudgery of the kitchen." ibid.

[211]Crummell (2000[orig.1851]), p. 60.

[212]Harper (1981[orig.1838]), p. 89.

[213]Spiegel (1996), p. 118, note 27.

[214]Thomas (1984), p. 299.

[215]*An address to the Negroes in the state of New-York* (1787) by Jupiter Hammon, servant of John Lloyd, http://etext.lib.virginia.edu/readex/20400.html (May 16, 2006).

[216]See Augustine's *City of God*, book XIX chapter 15, www.newadvent.org/fathers/120119.htm (May 16, 2006).

[217]www.biblestudylessons.com/cgi-bin/gospel_way/animal_meat.php (January 30, 2006).

[218]Hayes (1998), p. 84.

[219]"On the Third Article," in *The Twelve Articles of the Swabian Peasants* (1525) www.cas.sc.edu/hist/faculty/edwardsk/hist101S/reader/12art.html (May 3, 2005); and *Admonition to Peace: A Reply to the Twelve Articles of the Peasants in Swabia* (1525): www.wls.wels.net (May 23, 2006).

[220]www.openrescue.org/rescues/20020226/2002_02_26.html

[221]Harper (1981[orig.1838]), p. 89.

[222]Harper (1981[orig.1838]), p. 78.

[223]Hammond (1981[orig.1845]), p. 176.

[224]Hammond (1981[orig.1845]), p. 175.

[225]Stringfellow (1981[orig.1841]), p. 153.

[226]For an American context, see Angelina E. Grimké, *Appeal To The Christian Women of the South* (1836) and Walther (2005[orig.1863]) [an unpaginated electronic work]. The British abolitionists John Wesley and William Wilberforce were also accused of fanaticism. See Davis (1966), p. 383; and Hochschild (2004) [an unpaginated electronic work], respectively.

[227]Johnson (1988), p. 438.

[228]Johnson (1988), p. 438.

[229]Hammond (1981[orig.1845]), p. 175.

[230]*De Bow's Review*, "Slavery and the Bible" (1850), in Finkelman, ed. (2003), p. 114. See Philemon 12.

[231]Harper (1981[orig.1838]), p. 83.

[232]Walther (2005[orig.1863]) [an unpaginated electronic work].

[233]Walther (2005[orig.1863]), see e.g. note 6.

[234]Douglass (2005[orig.1855]) [an unpaginated electronic work].

[235]"Animal Rights' Hate-Crime Snafu," Salt Lake City Weekly, 5, July 2001, www.slweekly.com/editorial/2001/city_010705.cfm (May 5, 2006).

[236]www.withchrist.org/peta.htm (May 5, 2006)

[237]*Holy Cows* (2005), p. 42.

[238]www.withchrist.org/peta.htm (May 5, 2006)

[239]"Taming Beasts," Christianity Today, April, 2003 www.christianitytoday.com/ct/2003/004/37.120.html (May 5, 2006).

[240]Giacomo Cardinal Biffi, "Soloviev And Our Time," (2000), www.catholicculture.org/docs/doc_view.cfm?recnum=3430&longdesc (May 17, 2006).

[241]Hammond (1981[orig.1845]), p. 203.

[242]From Stuart's pamphlet, *Conscience and the Constitution* (1850), quoted on http://www.yaleslavery.org/WhoYaleHonors/stuart.html (April 28, 2006).

[243]From Robinson's *Slavery, As Recognized in the Mosaic Civil Law, Recognized Also, and Allowed, in the Abrahamic, Mosaic, and Christian Church* (1865), quoted in Bacon McClish (2005).

[244]Bacon McClish (2005). A version of this argument was used by the Methodist Dr. Nathan Bangs, in a text from 1834. Bangs opposed slavery but didn't think that Christians should be involved in abolitionism, since it divided the church. "When Jesus Christ sent out his Apostles to preach, did he give them a command to denounce those masters because they held slaves? and to tell them that unless they let those oppressed go free, they could not repent and enter the kingdom of heaven? Nothing of this." Quoted in Beals (1997), p. 60.

[245]Stringfellow (1981[orig.1841]), p. 155.

[246]Eastman (2000[orig.1852]), p. 298.

[247]Luke 17:7–8 (NIV). Jennifer A. Glancy writes that Jesus' parables "promote the view that the moral purpose of the slave is to advance the interests of the slaveholder." Glancy (2002), p. 129.

[248]Hammond (1981[orig.1845]), p. 174.

[249]Green (2005[orig.1839]).

[250]Angelina E. Grimké, *Appeal To The Christian Women of the South* (1836), http://history.furman.edu/~benson/docs/grimke2.htm (April 26, 2006). Compare with Luke 4:18 (King James): "The Spirit of the Lord is upon me, because he hath anointed me to preach the gospel to the poor; he hath sent me to heal the brokenhearted, to preach deliverance to the captives, and recovering of sight to the blind, to set at liberty them that are bruised."

[251]*Holy Cows*, (2005), p. 8.

[252]See Kaufman & Braun (2004), p. 59; and Towns & Towns, eds. (2001), p. 28.

[253]Hochschild (2004) [an unpaginated electronic work].

[254]Hochschild (2004) [an unpaginated electronic work].

[255]From Ames's *The Spirit of Humanity* (1835), quoted in Scully (2002), p. 88.

[256]www.yaleslavery.org/Abolitionists/torrey.html (May 10, 2006).

[257]Mabee (1970), p. 268.

[258]Hugh Thomas, "The Branding (and Baptism) of Slaves," www.ralphmag.org/slave2.html (May 30, 2006).

[259]Hochschild (2005), p. 28.

[260]Amos 5:21, 23–24 (NIV).

[261]From John 10:10 (New Jerusalem); and a prayer by Hildegard of Bingen (1098–1179), quoted in *Befrielsen* (1993), p. 172.

[262]Barton (1980), p. 74.

[263]From an edited version of Evans' journal, published 1837, quoted in Gilbert (1986). Reginald Reynolds writes in his book *The Wisdom of John Woolman*, that Evans "abstained from animal food, as he did also from the use of leather and the skins of slaughtered beasts."

[264]Quoted in *Befrielsen* (1993), p. 172

[265]1 John 4:8 (NRSV).

[266]Coleridge (1960[orig.1798]), p. 20.

[267]Coleridge (1960[orig.1798]), p. 48.

[268]Coleridge (1960[orig.1798]), p. 90.

[269]From Schweitzer's *The Philosophy of Civilization*, quoted in Wynne-Tyson, ed. (1990), p. 462.

[270]Nicholson (1989), pp. 108–109. See also www.sunnahonline.com/ilm/audio/series/dprophet_02.htm (May 10, 2005).

[271]Nurbakhsh (1990), pp. 31-32. We first encountered these stories on Sufism and animals in Akers (2000), Chapter 14.

[272]Schimmel (1975), p. 208.

[273]Sharafuddin Maneri, quoted in Carse (1994), p. 187.

[274]Jeanrond (2001), p. 93.

[275]Jeanrond (2001), p. 93.

[276]Thomas (1984), p. 21. This story, from a Muslim perspective, can be found in Nurbakhsh (1989), pp. 28–29.

[277]Nurbakhsh (1989), p. 17

[278]Nurbakhsh (1983), p. 107.

[279]Nurbakhsh (1983), p. 93.

[280]Murray (1978), p. 380. From the legend Eustace (also known as Placidus): "As he studied [the stag], he saw between its antlers what looked like the holy cross, shining more brightly than the sun. Upon the cross was the image of Jesus Christ. Christ then spoke to Placidus through the stag's mouth, as once he hade spoken through the mouth of Balaam's ass. The Lord said: 'O Placidus, why are you pursuing me?'" Stouck, ed. (1999), p. 550. For more examples of saints disrupting hunts, see Harwood (1928), p. 12; and Glacken (1967), p. 310. Glacken writes: "This Christian hagiography may indeed be a form of protest against heartless killing of wild animals." (p. 346).

[281]Lecky (1955), p. 169.

[282]"In the Bible the words translated as conversion – Hebrew *shub*; Greek: *epistrephein, strephein* and *metanoia* – mean merely to turn, to turn again, or to return." "Conversion" in Richardson & Bowden, eds. (1989), *A New Dictionary of Christian Theology*.

[283]See e.g. Jeremiah 7:5. In Luke 3:11, John the Baptist says: "The man with two tunics should share with him who has none, and the one who has food should do the same."

[284]"St. Benno and the Frog," in Waddell, ed. (1995), pp. 71–72; and Daniel 3:79, 81 (New Jerusalem).

[285]From Weil's *Waiting for God*, quoted in Stephen R. L. Clark, "The Covenant with All Living Creatures," www.all-creatures.org/articles/an-tpr-cov-hope.html (May 30, 2006).

[286]Mark 8:34 (NIV).

[287]"Towards Happier Meals In A Globalized World," www.worldwatch.org/press/news/2005/09/29 (March 31, 2006).

[288]About the events at the inn, see Buber (1975), p. 245. For a short biographical text, see "Zusya of Annopol" in Encyclopedia of Hasidim (1996), p. 563.

[289]Ryder (1989), p. 101.

[290]Quoted in Nibert (2002), p. 160.

[291]Jokkala & Strindlund (2003), p. 197.

[292]Jeremiah 8:11 (NIV).

[293]Quoted in Paul Shapiro, "The Myth of the Happy Farmed Animal," www.cok.net/inthenews/myth.php (May 22, 2006).

[294]www.astrazeneca.se/forskning/djur_policy.asp?printer-friendly=yes (January 30, 2006).

[295]www.arlafoods.dk, "Køernes trivsel" (June 3, 2006).

[296]Engström (2005), p. 31.

[297]Singer (1998), p. 373.

[298]Singer (1998), p. 383.

[299]Singer (1979), p. 108. For more on the animal ethics presented in Singer's books, see Patterson (2002), chapter 7.

[300]P1 (Programme One), Swedish National Public Radio, September 7, 2004.

[301]Sax (2000), p. 162.

[302]Thomas (1984), p. 298.

[303]Tolstoy (1988[orig. 1892]), p. 195.

[304]Kundera (1985), p. 281.

[305]Hochschild (2004) [an unpaginated electronic work].

[306]Singer (1998), p. 143.

[307]Singer (1998), p. 144.

[308]Linton (1997), p. 2. At a 1999 conference, a Swedish meat industry representative said that people need to think of meat as something that grows on trees. "When I sink my teeth into a pork chop, I for one don't want to think about how the animal was treated." Quoted in Engström (2000), p. 7.

[309]Marcus (2005), p. 121.

[310]Friedrich, "Veganism in a Nutshell: Conclusion," www.goveg.com (February 1, 2006).

[311]www.psyeta.org/sa/sa5.3/Arluke.html (May 15, 2006).

[312]Lyman (1974), p. 88.

[313]Singer & Burgin (1985), p. 152.

[314]Randour (2000), p. 40.

[315]Hollsing (2004), pp. 23–24.

[316]Hollsing (2004), p. 24.

[317]Barton (1980), pp. 71–72.

[318]Barton (1980), p. 74. We first read this story in Kowalski (1999), pp. 152–153.

[319]From Suttner's Schach der Qual (1898), quoted in Linnemann, ed. (2000), p. 248.

[320]Jensen (1993), p. 188.

[321]Merriam-Webster's Medical Dictionary (2002).

[322]Dictionary of the Swedish National Encyclopedia (Nationalencyclopedin).

[323]American Heritage Dictionary of the English Language, Fourth Edition (2000).

[324]Nurbakhsh (1983), p. 98. According to one Sufi story, Noah exclaimed upon seeing a dog: "How ugly this dog is! How unpleasant is its face!" God reproached him immediately: "O Noah, do you criticize Our creation? Are you better than him?" Noah wept. Nurbakhsh (1989), p. 7

[325]Nurbakhsh (1983), p. 99.

[326]Khalidi (2001), p. 122.

[327]Saint Isaac writes that the "charitable heart" burns "with charity for the whole of creation, for men, for the birds, for the beasts, for the demons–for all creatures. He who has such a heart cannot see or call to mind a creature without his eyes becoming filled with tears by reason of the immense compassion which seizes his heart; a heart which is softened and can no longer bear to see or learn from others of any suffering, even the smallest pain, being inflicted upon a creature. This is why such a man never ceases to pray also for the animals, for the enemies of Truth, and for those who do him evil, that they may be preserved and purified. He will pray even for the reptiles, moved by the infinite pity which reigns in the hearts of those who are becoming united to God." Quoted in Lossky (1957), p. 111. Isaac is an influential figure in Orthodox Christianity. Compare with Saint Silouan the Athonite, who wrote more than a thousand years later that "the Spirit of God teaches love toward all, and the soul feels compassion for every being, loves even her enemies and pities even devils because they have fallen away from the good." Archimandrite Sophrony (1991), p. 469.

[328]Archimandrite Sophrony (1991), p. 469.

[329]Keith Thomas writes of Meslier: "His sensibilities towards the sufferings of animals were so great as to lead him to atheism, on the grounds that the natural order was demonstrably imperfect if it could permit such cruelty." Thomas (1984), p. 182. See also Dommanget (1965), p. 62. This virtue is also found in fictional characters. The Bishop of Digne, one of the heroes of Victor Hugo's classic novel *Les Misérable*, is described as having an "excess of love," showing mercy even toward "a very large spider, black, hairy, and repellent." Hugo (1982[orig.1862]), pp. 65–66.

[330]Wisdom 11:24 (New Jerusalem).

[331]Quoted in "Thomas Aquinas – animal friendly?" The Ark Number 189, Winter 2001, www.all-creatures.org/ca/ark-189aquinas.html (January 19, 2006).

[332]Kean (1998), p. 111.

[333]Matthew 7:12 (NIV).

[334]From Harvey K. McArthur's "Golden Rule," in *A New Dictionary of Christian Ethics*, Macquarrie & Childress, eds. (1986), p. 251.

[335]Quoted in Magel, ed. (1989), p. 75.

[336]www.linnaeus.uu.se/online/ide/9_0.html (August 27, 2005).

[337]From Daggett's *The Rights of Animals: An Oration*, quoted in Clarke & Linzey, eds. (1990), p. 131.

[338]Thomas (1984), p. 291.

[339]From Chrysostom's homily XXVII on 1 Corinthians, quoted in the *Catechism of the Catholic Church* #1397.

[340]*Catechism of the Catholic Church* #1397.

[341]"St. Macarius of Alexandria and the Greatful Hyaena," in Waddell, ed. (1995), p. 15.

[342]Here is a classic example: The citizens of Gubbio, Italy wanted to kill a wolf that had repeatedly preyed on their livestock. Upon hearing this, Francis of Assisi sought out "Brother Wolf" and proposed a compromise. The people of Gubbio would provide him with a daily meal, and in exchange he would not harm any human or animal. According to the legend, the wolf placed his right paw in Francis's hand to close the deal. "What is extraordinary in the incident of the wolf of Gubbio is not that the wolf grew tame," writes the Italian hermit Carlo Carretto (1910–89), "but that the people of Gubbio grew tame, and that they ran to meet the cold and hungry wolf not with pruning knives and hatchets, but with bread and hot porridge." Carretto (1983), p. 108. See also *The Little Flowers of St Francis*, chap. 21, in Armstrong; Hellmann; & Short, eds. (2001), pp. 601–603.

[343]Dostoevsky (1991[orig.1879]), p. 295. Compare with the following passage from *The Life of St.*

Sergius: "In particular a bear used to come to the holy man . . . At this time Sergius had no variety of foods in the wilderness, only bread and water from the spring, and a great scarcity of these. Often, bread was not to be found; then both he and the bear went hungry. Sometimes, although there was but one slice of bread, the saint gave it to the bear, being unwilling to disappoint him of his food." www.st-sergius.org (February 6, 2006).

[344]Ellverson (2003), p. 145.

[345]Randour (2000), p. 63–64.

[346]Psalms 145:15–16 (New Jerusalem). See also Psalms 104: 27–28.

[347]P1 (Programme One), Swedish National Public Radio, January 11, 2005.

[348]Isaiah 2:4 (NIV).

[349]Micah 4:4 (NIV).

[350]Tolstoy (2005[orig.1896]).

[351]Bishop Kallistos of Diokleia, "The Liturgy After the Liturgy" www.incommunion.org/articles/older-issues/go-forth-in-peace (April 25, 2006).

[352]John Paul II (2005[orig.1979]) [an unpaginated electronic work].

[353]For a vegetarian perspective on the Dukhobours, see Spencer (1994), pp. 288–290. For a pacifist perspective, see Brock (1972), pp. 446–451. See also "Iskra," a contemporary Canadian Doukhobor magazine www.iskra.ca (May 15, 2006).

[354]Brock (1970), p. 105.

[355]On the Christian roots of the British campaign agaist cruely to animals, see Thomas (1984), p. 180. On Broome, see Andrew Linzey's entry "Broome, Arthur" in Bekoff, ed. (1998).

[356]Kean (1998), p. 110.

[357]"Quaker Views – Our Sense of Responsibility," www.quaker.org.uk (May 10, 2006).

[358]www.aktion-kirche-und-tiere.de (May 31, 2006); and Michael Blanke, "Church and Animals: An Urgent Issue," www.dike.de/akut/Texte/vortrag01.htm (May 4, 2006).

[359]Christian Vegetarian Association Update (electronic newsletter), February 12, 2006.

[360]1 John 4:16 (NRSV).

[361]"St. Ciaran and Brother Fox and Brother Badger," in Waddel, ed. (1995), pp. 101–106. We modernized the English.

[362]Fogelklou (1937), p. 261. The Bible passage is Revelation 21:5 (NRSV).

[363]Jeanrond (1995), p. 80.

[364]Mark 3:1–4 (Scholars).

[365]Borg (1998), p. 149.

[366]Luke 6:36 (New Jerusalem). For examples of Jesus' compassion, see Luke 7:13; Mark 6:34; & Matthew 9:36.

[367]See Borg (1998), chap. 5.

[368]Elyse Bell, personal communication, February 10, 2006.

[369]From *The Trumpet Call* (17th Issue, 1995), published by the Peniel Pentecostal Church, quoted in Linzey (1998), p. 55.

[370]Psalms 104:24, 29–30 (NIV).

[371]Wisdom 11:26–12:1 (New Jerusalem).

[372]Enquist (2005), pp. 75–76. The original English translation contains an error that we have corrected.

[373]From Tolstoy's essay *The First Step* (1892), quoted in Preece, ed. (2002), p. 299.

[374]Jeanrond (2001), p. 18.

[375]Bauckham (1998a), pp. 38–39.

[376]Bauckham (1998a), p. 261, note 25.

[377]www.nazarene.net/enoch/2enoch01-68.htm#Chapter58 (May 10, 2005).

[378]Dahlstrand (1996), p. 56.

[379]Blake, "Auguries of Innocence," www.sanjeev.net/poetry/blake-william/index.html (June 3, 2006). In Lagerlöf's *The Wonderful Adventures of Nils*, a masterpiece of children's literature, a boy disappears and his anguished parents wonder if it is God's punishment for their work to have a nearby lake drained. The mother realizes that draining a lake that is home to so many birds would be a "cruel act." The narrator writes that the "anguish which she herself was suffering opened her heart. She felt that she was not so far removed from all other living creatures as people usually think." The husband reflects, "It may be that God does not want us to interfere with His order." Lagerlöf (1995[orig. 1906–07]), pp. 207–208. Coetzee's novel *Disgrace* contains this dialogue between the protagonist David Lurie and a woman at an animal clinic:

"Do I like animals? I eat them, so I suppose I must like them, some parts of them."

"Yes, we eat a lot of animals in this country," she says. "It doesn't seem to do us much good. I'm not sure how we will justify it to them."

Justify it? When? At the Great Reckoning? He would be curious to hear more, but this is not the time." Coetzee (2000), p. 82.

[380]Quoted in "Thomas Aquinas – animal friendly?" The Ark Number 189, Winter 2001, www.all-creatures.org/ca/ark-189aquinas.html (January 19, 2006).

[381]For the original medieval text, see *Dives and Pauper* (1980), p. 35. For a modernized version, see Preece, ed. (2002), p. 90. For more information about the treatise, see Thomas (1984), p. 153.

[382]Wisdom 5:17 (New Jerusalem). In *Dives and Pauper*, the verse reads: "he schal armyn / creaturys in venchance of his enmyss," a translation of the Latin "Armabit creaturam in ulcionem inimicorum." Dives and Pauper (1980), p. 35.

[383]Jeffrey L. Hawkins, "Advice from Farm Country" in *Creation Care* magazine Spring 2005, www.creationcare.org (February 7, 2006). This utilitarian view is not new. The influential Puritan Cotton Mather (1666–1728) declared "what is not useful is vicious." His sermons, writes Jim Mason, "put forth the zeitgeist for colonial America. His remark sums up the views of agrarian civilizations toward animals and nature." Mason (2005), p. 158.

[384]See "Drewermann, Eugen," www.tierrechteportal.de/Bibliothek (February 7, 2006).

[385]Jangfeldt (2003), p. 121.

[386]Munthe (1929), pp. 527–528. A parallel scene can be found in Francis Jammes's "The Paradise of Beasts," in Romance of the Rabbit (1903). A horse dies and reaches the gate of heaven.

"A great scholar, who was waiting for St. Peter to come and open the gate, said to the horse:

'What are you doing here? You have no right to enter heaven. I have the right because I was born of a woman.'

And the poor horse answered:

'My mother was a gentle mare. She died in her old age with her blood sucked out by leeches. I have come to ask the Bon Dieu if she is here.'

Then the gate of Heaven was opened to the two who knocked upon it, and the Paradise of animals appeared.

And the old horse recognized his mother, and she recognized him."

Jammes (2004[orig.1903]).

[387] Munthe (1929), p. 530.

[388] "The Mountains That are Creatures of God," in Waddell, ed. (1995), pp. 134–136.

[389] Lehane (1993), p. 66.

[390] Power Bratton (1993), p. 193.

[391] Merton (2001), p. 263.

[392] Merton (2001), p. 111.

[393] Quoted in "Unlived Life: A Manifesto Against Factory Farming," (Campaigners Against Factory Farming, 1966) quoted in Wynne-Tyson, ed. (1990), p. 302.

— Works Cited —

Adomnán of Iona (1995[orig.690]). *Life of St Columba*. London: Penguin Books.

Akers, Keith (2000). *The Lost Religion of Jesus: Simple Living and Nonviolence in Early Christianity*. New York: Lantern Books.

Aigus, Ambrose (1970). *God's Animals*. London: Catholic Study Circle for Animal Welfare.

Andrén, Olof, ed. (1994). *Evangeliets gryning*. Uppsala: Pro Veritate.

Archimandrite Sophrony (1991). *Saint Silouan the Athonite*. Crestwood, New York: St Vladimir's Seminary Press.

Attwater, Donald (1960). *St John Chrysostom: Pastor and Preacher*. London: The Catholic Book Club.

Regis J. Armstrong; J. Wayne Hellmann; & William J. Short, eds. (2000). *Francis of Assisi: Early Documents. Vol. 2: The Founder*. Hyde Park, NY: New City Press.

—. (2001). *Francis of Assisi: Early Documents. Vol. 3: The Prophet*. Hyde Park, NY: New City Press.

Bacon McClish, Jacqueline (2005). "From Slavery to Sexuality: Putting Arguments from Scripture into Historical Context" (Presentation to Integrity Austin April 17, 1999). www.geocities.com/austin-tegrity/From_Slavery_to_Sexuality.htm (May 29, 2005).

Barton, Clara (1980). *The Story of My Childhood*. New York: Arno Press.

Bartov, Omer & Mack, Phyllis, eds. (2001). *In God's Name: Genocide and Religion in the Twentieth Century*. New York: Berghahn Books.

Bastaire, Hélène & Jean (1996). *Le chant des créatures: Les chrétiens et l'univers d'Irénée à Claudel*. Paris: Cerf.

Bauckham, Richard (1994). "Jesus and the Wild Animals (1 Mark 1:13): A Christological Image for an Ecological Age," in Green & Turner, eds. (1994), pp. 3-21.

—. (1998a). "Jesus and Animals I: What did he Teach?," in Linzey & Yamamoto, eds. (1998), pp. 33-48.

—. (1998b). "Jesus and Animals II: What did he Practise?," in Linzey & Yamamoto, eds. (1998), pp. 49-60.

Beals, Ivan A. (1997). *Our Racist Legacy: Will The Church Resolve The Conflict?* CrossRoads Books.

Befrielsen (1993). Stockholm: Svenska kyrkans centralstyrelse/Verbum.

Bekoff, Marc, ed. (1998). *Encyclopedia of Animal Rights and Animal Welfare*. Westport, Connecticut: Greenwood Press.

Bergen, Doris L. (1996). *Twisted Cross: The German Christian Movement in the Third Reich*. Chapel Hill: The University of North Carolina Press.

Bergmann, Sigurd (2005). *Creation Set Free: The Spirit as Liberator of Nature*. Grand Rapids, Michigan: William B. Eerdmans Publishing Company.

Bernhard, Joseph (1937). *Heilige und Tiere*. Munich: Verlag Ars Sacra Josef Müller.

Beskow, Per (1983). *Strange Tales about Jesus: A Survey of Unfamiliar Gospels*. Philadelphia, Pennsylvania: Fortress Press.

Bieringer, R., Pollefeyt, D., & Vandecasteele-Vanneuville, F, eds. (2001). *Anti-Judaism and the Fourth Gospel: Papers of the Leuven Colloquium*. Assen: Royal Van Gorcum.

Birgitta (1958). *Himmelska uppenbarelser.* Andra bandet. Malmö: Allhems förlag.

Bonhoeffer, Dietrich (1997). *Creation and Fall: A Theological Exposition of Genesis 1-3.* Minneapolis: Fortress Press.

Borg, Marcus J. (1998). *Conflict, Holiness and Politics in the Teachings of Jesus.* Harrisburg, PA: Trinity Press International.

Brekus, Catherine A. (2001). "Children of Wrath, Children of Grace: Jonathan Edwards and the Puritan Culture of Child Rearing," in Bunge, ed. (2001), pp. 300-328.

Brock, Peter (1970). *Twentieth-Century Pacifism.* New York: Van Nostrand Reinhold Company.

–. (1972). *Pacifism in Europe to 1914.* New Jersey: Princeton University Press.

Brueggemann, Walter (1982). *Genesis: A Bible Commentary for Teaching and Preaching.* Atlanta: John Knox Press.

Buber, Martin (1975). *Tales of the Hasidim: The Early Masters.* New York: Schocken Books.

Bunge, Marcia J., ed. (2001). *The Child in Christian Thought.* Grand Rapids, Michigan: William B. Eerdmans Publishing Company.

Bönboken (2003). Stockholm: Verbum.

Carretto, Carlo (1983). *I, Francis.* London: HarperCollings.

Carse, James P. (1994). *Breakfast at the Victory: The Mysticism of Ordinary Experience.* New York: Harper Collins.

Cassuto, Umberto (1961). *A Commentary on the Book of Genesis. Part 1. From Adam to Noah.* Jerusalem: The Magnes Press.

–. (1964). *A Commentary on the Book of Genesis. Part 2. From Noah to Abraham.* Jerusalem: The Magnes Press.

Claesson, Bo (2000). *Erfarenhet, tro, handling.* University of Gothenburg, Sweden.

Clarke, Paul A.B. & Linzey, Andrew, eds. (1990). *Political Theory And Animal Rights.* London: Pluto Press

Clément, Olivier (2002). "Djuren i den ortodoxa tanken II," *Signum* no. 1/2002, pp. 44-50.

Cluysenaar, Anne & Schwenk, Norman, eds. (2004). *The Hare That Hides Within: Poems about St. Melangell.* Cardigan: Parthian.

Cohn-Sherbok, Dan & Linzey, Andrew (1997) *After Noah: Animals and the Liberation of Theology.* London: Mowbray.

Coetzee, J.M. (2000). *Disgrace.* London: Vintage.

Corley, Kathleen (2002). *Women & the Historical Jesus: Feminist Myths of Christian Origins.* Santa Rosa, CA: Polebridge Press.

Crummell, Alexander (2000[orig.1851]). "An Address to the British Antislavery Society," in *Against Slavery: An Abolitionist Reader* (2000). London: Penguin, pp. 60-62.

Dahlstrand, Maximilian (1996). "Djurens ställning i olika trosriktningar och religioner: Islam," in *Kungl. Skogs- och Lantbruksakademiens tidskrift* no. 9/1996, pp. 53-57.

Davis, David Brion (1966). *The Problem of Slavery in Western Culture.* Ithaca, New York: Cornell University Press.

Davis, Oliver & Bowie, Fiona, eds. (1995). *Celtic Christian Spirituality: Medieval and Modern.* London: SPCK.

Deane-Drummond, Cecilia (2004). *The Ethics of Nature.* Malden: Blackwell.

deMause, Lloyd, ed. (1974). *The History of Childhood.* New York: The Psychohistory Press.

Dives and Pauper (1980). Volume 1, part 2. Edited by Priscilla Heath Barnum. Oxford: Oxford University Press.

Dommanget, Maurice (1965). *Le curé Meslier*. Paris: Les Lettres Nouvelles.

Dostoevsky, Fyodor (1991[orig.1879]). *The Brothers Karamazov*. New York: Vintage Books.

Douglass, Frederick (2005[orig.1855]). *My Bondage and My Freedom*. www.worldwideschool.org /library/books/hst/biography/MyBondageandMyFreedom/chap26.html (May 23, 2006).

Drane, John (1979). *Jesus and the four Gospels*. Herts: Lion Publishing.

Duckett, Eleanor (1959). *The Wandering Saints*. London: Collins.

Dunayer, Joan (2001). *Animal Equality: Language and Liberation*. Derwood: Ryce Publishing.

Eadmer (1962). *The Life of St Anselm, Archbishop of Canterbury/Vita Sancti Anselmi, archiepiscopi Cantuariensis*. London: Thomas Nelson and Sons Ltd.

Eastman, Mary (2000[orig.1852]). "Aunt Phillis's Cabin; or, Southern Life As It Is," in *Against Slavery: An Abolitionist Reader* (2000). London: Penguin, pp. 296-300.

Eckhart, Meister & Fox, Matthew (1991). *Breakthrough: Meister Eckhart's Creation Spirituality in New Translation*. New York: Image Books.

Einarsson, Tomas (2005). *Paradiset åter*. Skellefteå, Sweden: Artos.

Ellverson, Karl-Gunnar (2003). *Handbok i Liturgik*. Stockholm: Verbum.

Engström, Henrik (2000). "Korvar och kotletter växer på träden," in *Djurens rätt* no. 1/2000, p. 7.

–. (2005). "Må bra och trivas," in *Djurens rätt* no. 2/2005, p. 7.

Enquist, Per Olov (2005). *Lewi' Journey*. New York: Overlook Duckworth.

Eriksson, Anne-Louise, ed. (2004). *Tolkning för livet*. Stockholm: Verbum.

Eriksson, Anne-Louise; Grenholm, Christina; Jeanrond, Werner G.; Jonsson, Johnny; Lindström, Fredrik (2004). *Öppningar: Möten med bibeln*. Nora: Nya Doxa.

Faust, Drew Gilpin, ed. (1981). *The Ideology of Slavery: Proslavery Thought in the Antebellum South, 1830-1860*. Baton Rough and London: Louisiana State University Press.

Fiedler, Maureen & Rabben, Linda, eds. (1998). *Rome Has Spoken: A Guide to Forgotten Papal Statements, and How They Have Changed Through the Centuries*. New York: Crossroad.

Finkelman, Paul, ed. (2003). *Defending Slavery: Proslavery Thought in the Old South. A Brief History with Documents*. Boston/New York: Bedford/St. Martin's.

Fogelklou, Emilia (1937). *Protestant och katolik*. Stockholm: Albert Bonniers förlag.

Fox, Matthew (2000). *Original Blessing: A Primer in Creation Spirituality*. New York: Jeremy P. Tarcher/Putnam.

Frostin, Per (1970). *Kampen för rättfärdighet*. Stockholm: Wilhelmssons.

Gaffney, James (1998). "Can Catholic Morality Make Room for Animals?," in Linzey & Yamamoto, eds. (1998), pp. 100-112.

García-Rivera, Alex (1995). *St. Martín de Porres: The "Little Stories" and the Semiotics of Culture*. New York: Maryknoll.

Gilbert, Joan (1986). "Joshua Evans: Consistent Quaker," in *The Friendly Vegetarian*, No. 13, Spring 1986. www.vegetarianfriends.net/issue6.html#7 (May 18, 2005).

Glacken, Clarence J. (1967). *Traces on the Rhodian Shore. Nature and Culture in Western Thought From Ancient Times to the End of the Eighteenth Century*. Berkley & Los Angeles: University of California Press.

Glancy, Jennifer A. (2002). *Slavery in Early Christianity*. Oxford: Oxford University Press.

Green, Joel B. & Turner, Max (1994). *Jesus of Nazareth: Lord and Christ: Essays on the Historical Jesus and New Testament Christology.* Grand Rapids: William B. Eerdmans Publishing Company.

Gregory, James (2001). "A Michigander, a Patriot and Gentleman: H. S. Clubb, President of the American Vegetarian Society," Voices, Kancoll's Online Magazine, www.kancoll.org/voices_2001/0701gregory.htm (August 2, 2006).

Guiley, Rosemary (2001). *The Encyclopedia of Saints.* New York: Checkmark Books.

Gundry-Volf, Judith M. (2001). "The Least and the Greatest: Children in the New Testament," in Bunge, ed. (2001), pp. 29-60.

Gutiérrez, Gustavo (1988). *A Theology of Liberation.* London: SCM Press.

Habel, Norman C. (1985). *The Book of Job: A Commentary.* London: SCM Press Ltd.

Hamm, Thomas D. (1995). *God's Government Begun: The Society For Universal Inquiry and Reform, 1842-1846.* Bloomington and Indianapolis: Indiana University Press.

Hammar, KG (2000). *Ecce Homo.* Lund/Stockholm: Arcus/Verbum.

Hammond, James Henry (1981[orig.1845]). "Letter to an English Abolitionist," pp. 170-205 in Faust, ed. (1981).

Harper, William (1981[orig.1838]). "Memoir on Slavery," in Faust, ed. (1981), pp. 78-135.

Harwood, Dix (1928). *Love for Animals And How It Developed in Great Britain.* New York.

Hayes, Diana (1998). "Reflections on slavery," in Fielder & Rabben, eds. (1998), pp. 86-90.

Hays, Richard B. (1996). *The Moral Vision of the New Testament: A Contemporary Introduction to New Testament Ethics.* New York: HarperCollins Publishers.

Heschel, Susannah (2001). "When Jesus Was an Aryan: The Protestant Chuch and Antisemitic Propaganda," in Bartov & Mack, eds. (2001), pp. 79-101.

Hildegaard of Bingen (1996). *Secrets of God: Writings of Hildegard of Bingen.* (Selected and translated from the Latin by Sabina Flanagan). Boston & London: Shambhala.

Hill, Jim & Cheadle, Rand (1996). *The Bible Tells Me So: Uses and Abuses of Holy Scripture.* New York: Anchor Book.

Hochschild, Adam (2004). "Against All Odds," Mother Jones magazine January/February 2004, www.motherjones.com/news/feature/2004/01/12_403.html

–. (2005). *Bury The Chains: The British Struggle to Abolish Slavery.* London: Macmillan.

Hollsing, Ingmar (2004). "Erik Kallesson - vår 'äldste' medlem," in *Kväkartidskrift* no. 1/2004, pp. 21-29.

Holy Cows: How PETA twists religion to push animal "rights" (2005), www.consumerfreedom.com/downloads/pro/docs/050801_PetaReligion.pdf (January 28, 2006).

Hugo, Victor (1982[orig.1862]). *Les Misérables.* London: Penguin Books.

Iacobbo, Karen & Iacobbo, Michael (2004). *Vegetarian America: A History.* Westport: Praeger.

Jammes, Francis (2004[orig.1903]). *Romance of the Rabbit.* www.gutenberg.org/etext/12909 (January 31, 2006)

Jangfeldt, Bengt (2003). *En osalig ande: Berättelsen om Axel Munthe.* Stockholm: Wahlström & Widstrand.

Jeanrond, Werner (1995). *Call and Response: The Challenge of Christian Life.* Dublin: Gill & Macmillan.

–. (1998). *Guds närvaro.* Lund: Arcus.

–. (2001). *Gudstro.* Lund: Arcus.

Jensen, Per (1993). *Djurens beteende och orsakerna till det.* Stockholm: LTs förlag.

John Paul II. *Redemptor Hominis* (The Redeemer of Man) (2005[orig.1979].
http://us.catholic.net/RCC/documents/JohnPaulII/redemptor.html (den 22 januari 2005).

Jokkala, Toivo & Strindlund, Pelle (2003). *Djurrätt och socialism.* Göteborg: Lindelöws bokförlag.

Johnson, Elizabeth A. (1990). *Consider Jesus: Waves of Renewal in Christology.* London: Geoffrey Chapman.

Johnson, Paul (1988). *A History of Christianity.* London: Penguin Books.

Jónsson, Gunnlaugur A. (1988). *The Image of God: Genesis 1:26-28 in a Century of Old Testament Research.* Stockholm: Almqvist & Wiksell International.

Julian of Norwich (1966[orig.1373]). *Revelations of Divine Love.* Harmondsworth: Penguin Books.

Kaufman, Stephen R. & Braun, Nathan (2004). *Good News for All Creation: Vegetarianism as Christian Stewardship.* Cleveland, Ohio. Vegetarian Advocates Press.

Kean, Hilda (1998). *Animal Rights: Political and Social Change in Britain since 1800.* London: Reaktion Books.

Kempe, Margery (1985). *The Book of Margery Kempe.* Middlesex, England: Penguin Books.

Kowalski, Gary (1999). *The Souls of Animals.* Walpole: Stillpoint.

Khalidi, Tarif (2001). *The Muslim Jesus: Sayings and Stories in Islamic Literature.* Cambridge, Massachusetts: Harvard University Press.

Kundera, Milan (1985). *The Unbearable Lightness of Being.* London: Faber and Faber.

Lagerlöf, Selma (1995[orig. 1906-07]). *The Wonderful Adventures of Nils.* New York: Dover Publications.

Lay, Benjamin (2006[orig.1737]). *All Slave-keepers that keep the Innocent in Bondage, Apostates* (published by the author in Philadelphia). http://antislavery.eserver.org/religious/allslavekeepersfinal.doc (February 11, 2006).

Lecky, William Edward Hartpole (1955). *History of European Morals: From Augustus to Charlemagne.* New York: George Braziller.

Lederer, Susan E. (1995). *Subjected to Science: Human Experimentation in America before the Second World War.* Baltimore and London: The Johns Hopkins University Press.

Lehane, Brendan (1993). *Early Celtic Christianity.* New York: Barnes & Noble Books.

Libell, Monica (2001). *Morality Beyond Humanity: Schopenhauer, Grysanowski, and Schweitzer on Animal Ethics.* Lund: Avdelningen för Idé- och lärdomshistoria vid Lunds universitet.

Linnemann, Manuela, ed. (2000). *Brüder, Bestien, Automaten.* Erlangen: Harald Fischer Verlag.

Linton, Magnus (1997). "Intro: Bekväm moral," in *Arbetaren* no. 32/1997, p. 2.

Linzey, Andrew (1994). *Animal Theology.* London: SCM Press.

–. (1998). *Animal Gospel: Christian Faith As Though Animals Mattered.* London: Hodder & Stoughton.

–. (2000). "Good Causes Do Not Need Exaggeration," in *The Animals' Agenda*, January/February 2000, pp. 24-25.

Linzey, Andrew & Regan, Tom, eds. (1988). *Animals and Christianity: A Book of Readings.* New York: Crossroad.

Linzey, Andrew & Yamamoto, Dorothy, eds. (1998). *Animals on the Agenda.* London: SCM Press.

Lossky, Vladimir (1957). *The Mystical Theology of the Eastern Church.* Cambridge & London: James Clarke & Co. Ltd.

Lyman, Richard B. (1974). "Barbarism and Religion: Late Roman and Early Medieval Childhood," in deMause, Lloyd, ed. (1974), pp. 75-100.

Mabee, Carleton (1970). *Black Freedom: The Nonviolent Abolitionists from 1830 Through the Civil War*. London: Collier-Macmillan Limited.

Magel, Charles R., ed. (1989). *Keyguide to Information Sources in Animal Rights*. London: Mansell Publishing Limited.

Marcus, Erik (2005). *Meat Market: Animals, Ethics, & Money*. Boston: Brio Press.

Mason, Jim (2005). *An Unnatural Order: The Roots of Our Destruction of Nature*. Lantern Books: New York.

Macquarrie, John & Childress, James, eds. (1986). *A New Dictionary of Christian Ethics*. London: SCM Press.

Malaty, Tadros Y (1993). *Introduction to the Coptic Orthodox Church*. St George's Coptic Orthodox Church.

Meister Eckhart (1981). *The Essential Sermons, Commentaries, Treatises, and Defense*. Mahwah, NJ: Paulist Press.

Merton, Thomas (2001). *The Intimate Merton: His Life from His Journals*, edited by Patrick Hart and Jonathan Montaldo. HarperSanFrancisco.

–. (2003). *When the Trees Say Nothing: Writings on Nature*. Notre Dame, IN: Sorin Books.

Miller, Robert J., ed. (1994). *The Complete Gospels: Annotated Scholars Version*. Sonoma, CA: Polebridge Press.

Monahan, Joan (2002). *Martin de Porres: A Saint for Our Time*. New York: Paulist Press.

More, Thomas (1992[orig.1516]). *Utopia* [translated by Robert M. Adams]. New York: W.W. Norton & Company.

–. (2003[orig.1516]). *Utopia* [translated by Paul Turner]. London: Penguin Books.

Munthe, Axel (1929). *The Story of San Michele*. London: John Murray.

Murray, Alexander (1978). *Reason and Society in the Middle Ages*. Oxford: Clarendon Press.

Myers, Ched; Dennis, Marie; Nangle, Joseph; Moe-Lobeda, Cynthia & Taylor, Stuart (1996). *"Say to this Mountain": Mark's Story of Discipleship*. New York: Orbis Books.

Mäster Eckehart (1961). *Predikningar*. Stockholm: Natur och Kultur.

Nibert, David (2002). *Animal Rights/Human Rights: Entanglements of Oppression and Liberation*. Lanham, Maryland: Rowman & Littlefield.

Nicholson, Reynold A. (1989). *The Mystics of Islam*. London: Arkana.

Nurbakhsh, Javad (1983). *Jesus in the Eyes of the Sufis*. London: Khaniqahi-Nimatullahi Publications.

–. (1989). *Dogs from a Sufi Point of View*. London: Khaniqahi-Nimatullahi Publications.

–. (1990). *Sufi Women*. London: Khaniqahi-Nimatullahi Publications.

Palmdahl, Marika (2005). *Det nya landet*. Lund: Arcus.

Patterson, Charles (2002). *Eternal Treblinka: Our Treatment of Animals and the Holocaust*. New York: Lantern Books.

Phelps, Norm (2002a). *Love For All Creatures: Frequently Asked Questions about the Bible and Animal Rights*. www.fundforanimals.org/library/documentViewer.asp?ID=640&table=documents (February 7, 2006).

–. (2002b). *The Dominion of Love: Animal Rights According to the Bible*. New York: Lantern Books.

Pierce, Brian J (2004). *Martin de Porres: A Saint of the Americas*. Liguori: Liguori Publications.

Power Bratton, Susan (1988). "The Original Desert Solitaire: Early Christian Monasticism and Wilderness," in Enviromental Ethics, Spring 1988, Volume 10, Number 1, pp. 31-53.

—. (1993). *Christianity, Wilderness, and Wildlife: The Original Desert Solitaire*. Scranton: University of Scranton Press.

Preece, Rod & Fraser, David (2000). "The Status of Animals in Biblical and Christian Thought: A Study in Colliding Values" in *Society & Animals Journal of Human-Animal Studies*, volume 8, Number 3, 2000, www.psyeta.org/sa/sa8.3/fraser.shtml (July 7, 2005).

Preece, Rod, ed. (2002). *Awe for the Tiger, Love for the Lamb: A Chronicle of Sensibility to Animals*. Vancouver: University of British Columbia Press.

Randour, Mary Lou (2000). *Animal Grace: Entering A Spiritual Relationship with Our Fellow Creatures*. Novato, California: New World Library.

Robson, Michael (1999). *St. Francis of Assisi: The Legend and the Life*. London: Continuum.

Rollin, Bernard E. (1990). *The Unheeded Cry: Animal Consciousness, Animal Pain and Science*. Oxford: Oxford University Press.

Rowley, H. H. (1980). *Job*. Grand Rapids: William B. Eerdmans Publishing Company.

Ryder, Richard (1989). *Animal Revolution: Changing Attitudes Towards Speciesism*. Oxford: Basil Blackwell.

Saint Gregory Nazianzen (1986). *Selected Poems*. Translated with an introduction by John McGuckin. Oxford: SLG Press.

Saramago, José (1994). *The Gospel According to Jesus Christ*. San Diego, CA: Harcourt Brace & Company.

Sax, Boria (2000). *Animals in the Third Reich: Pets, Scapegoats, and the Holocaust. New York: Continuum.

Schimmel, Annemarie (1975). *Mystical Dimensions of Islam*. Chapel Hill: University of North Carolina Press.

Scully, Matthew (2002). *Dominion: The Power of Man, the Suffering of Animals, and the Call to Mercy*. New York: St. Martin's Press.

Shinn, Roger L. (1986). "Slavery," in Macquarrie & Childress, eds. (1986), pp. 589-590.

Singer, Isaac Bashevis (1979). "Pigeons," *A Friend of Kafka and Others Stories*. New York: Penguin Books, pp. 107-117.

—. (1998). *Shadows on the Hudson*. New York: Farrar, Straus and Giroux.

Singer, Isaac Bashevis & Burgin, Richard (1985). *Conversations with Isaac Bashevis Singer*. New York: Doubleday & Company.

Singer, Peter (1990). *Animal Liberation*. New York: Avon Books.

—. (1993). *Practical Ethics*. Cambridge: Cambridge University Press.

—. (1998). *Ethics Into Action: Henry Spira and the Animal Rights Movement*. Lanham, Maryland: Rowman & Littlefield.

Sorabji, Richard (1993). *Animal Minds and Human Morals: The Origins of the Western Debate*. Ithaca: Cornell University Press.

Sorrell, Roger D. (1988). *St. Francis of Assisi and Nature: Tradition and Innovation in Western Christian Attitudes toward the Enviroment*. Oxford: Oxford University Press.

Spencer, Colin (1994). *The Heretic's Feast: A History of Vegetarianism*. London: Fourth Estate.

Spiegel, Marjorie (1996). *The Dreaded Comparison: Human and Animal Slavery*. New York: Mirror Books.

Stendahl, Krister (2004). "Förord," in Eriksson, ed. (2004), pp. 7-9.

Stouck, Mary-Ann, ed. (1999). *Medieval Saints: A Reader*. Peterborough, Ont.; Orchard Park, NY: Broadview Press.

Stringfellow, Thornton (1981[orig.1841]). "A Brief Examination of Scripture Testimony on the Institution of Slavery," in Faust, ed. (1981), pp. 138-167.

Ström, Ingmar (1983). *Glädjebudet enligt Markus*. Älvsjö: Verbum.

Svartvik, Jesper (2001). "Den äldsta långdistansmissilen," in *Skriftens ansikten*. Lund: Arcus, pp. 66-91.

–. (2004). "Vem vaktar väktarna?," in Eriksson ed. (2004), pp. 168-192.

The New Interpreter's Bible: Volume I (1994). Nashville: Abingdon Press.

Thomas, Keith (1984). *Man and the Natural World: Changing Attitudes in England 1500-1800*. London: Penguin Books.

Tolstoj, Leo (1988[orig. 1892]), *The First Step*, in Linzey & Regan, eds. (1988), pp. 194-197.

–. (2005[orig.1896]). "Letter to Ernest Howard Crosby," www.myspot.org/tolstoy/crosby.html (December 12, 2005).

Towns, Sharon & Towns, Daniel, eds. (2001). *Voices from the Garden: Stories of Becoming a Vegetarian*. New York: Lantern Books.

Tuchman, Barbara W. (1979). *A Distant Mirror: The Calamitous 14th Century*. London: Macmillan.

Turner, E.S. (1992). *All Heaven in a Rage*. Fontwell: Centaur Press.

Van de Weyer, ed. (1990). *Celtic Fire: An Anthology of Celtic Christian Literature*. London: Darton, Longman and Todd.

von Rad, Gerhard (1972). *Genesis: A Commentary*. The Westminister Press. Philadelphia.

Waddel, Helen, ed. (1995). *Beasts and Saints*. London: Constable and Company Ltd.

Walther, C.F.W (2005[orig.1863]). *Slavery, Humanism, and the Bible: Selections from Lehre und Wehre by C.F.W. Walther*. www.reclaimingwalther.org/articles/cfw00002.htm (April 12, 2005).

Watner, Carl (1982). "Charles Lane: Voluntaryist." http://users.aol.com/vlntryst/clintro.html (August 8, 2006).

Wenham, Gordon J. (1987). *Genesis 1-15*. Waco, Texas: Word Biblical Commentary.

Westermann, Claus (1984). *Genesis 1-11: A Commentary*. London: SPCK.

Wink, Walter (2003). *Jesus and Nonviolence: A Third Way*. Minneapolis: Fortress Press.

Woolman, John (1909[orig.1774]). *The Journal of John Woolman*. Charlottesville, New York: P F Collier & Son, ebook at University of Virginia Library, www.netlibrary.com.ezproxy.ub.gu.se/Details.aspx (eBook ISBN: 0585209561).

Wynne-Tyson, Jon, ed. (1990). *The Extended Circle: An Anthology of Humane Thought*. London: Cardinal.

— ACKNOWLEDGEMENTS —

Every Creature a Word of God is a revised and expanded version of a book originally published in Swedish, *Varje varelse ett Guds ord: Omsorg om djuren som kristen andlighet*. That book came out in 2005 from the Arcus publishing house in Lund, Sweden.

For the English version, we are grateful for the assistance of Stephen Kaufman, M.D., chair of the Christian Vegetarian Association and co-author of *Good News for All Creation*. He was an attentive reader of the manuscript and provided us with many insightful comments. We are also grateful for his belief in the book — a constant source of encouragement.

Our friend and fellow peace activist Joel Kilgour took time off from living and working with the down-and-out of Duluth, Minnesota to come to Sweden and help us translate the book. Not only did he render our thoughts into fine English prose, but as a skilled lay theologian he offered valuable comments on nearly every page. We are thus indebted to him for both form and content, and we gratefully dedicate *Every Creature a Word of God* to Joel.

— ABOUT THE AUTHORS —

ANNIKA SPALDE (1969-) is an ordained deacon in the Church of Sweden (Lutheran) and a founding member of the Swedish Christian Vegetarian Movement. Her work for nonviolence and justice has included participation in the Trident Ploughshares campaign to abolish the British nuclear arsenal; organizing against the Swedish arms industry; serving as an Ecumenical Accompanier in Israel/Palestine; working as an assistant nurse in Paraguay; and living with the homeless at a Catholic Worker house in Duluth, Minnesota.

PELLE STRINDLUND (1971-) holds an MA in Religious Studies and is a founding member of The Rescue Service, a Swedish animal rights organization working with nonviolent civil disobedience. His commitment to justice and peace has led him to volunteer as a social worker in Tyler, Texas; live with threatened indigenous villagers in Guatemala; and accompany harassed children to and from school in Palestine.

Spalde and Strindlund met through their work for nuclear disarmament. They are married and live in Gothenburg, on Sweden's west coast. They have previously published a book on Christian nonviolence.

The authors can be contacted at info@viacordis.se.

* * *

Printed in the United States
203265BV00010B/1-27/P

9 780971 667631